HAPPYBABY HAPPYYOU

500 Ways to Nurture the Bond with Your Baby

KARYN SIEGEL-MAIER

Storey

The mission of Storey Publishing is to serve our customers by publishing practical information that encourages personal independence in harmony with the environment.

Edited by Lisa H. Hiley
Art direction by Alethea Morrison
Cover and book design by Jessica Hische
Indexed by Nancy D. Wood

Text © 2009 by Karyn Seigel-Maier
Illustrations © 2009 by Jessica Hische

Printed in the United States by Versa Press
10 9 8 7 6 5 4 3 2 1

Library of Congress Cataloging-in-Publication Data

Siegel-Maier, Karyn, 1960–
  Happy baby, happy you / by Karyn Siegel-Maier.
     p. cm.
  Includes index.
  ISBN 978-1-60342-141-6 (pbk. : alk. paper)
  1. Infants—Care. 2. Newborn infants—Care.
  3. Parenting. 4. Child care. I. Title.
HQ774.S545 2009
649'.122—dc22

                                    2009001480

To mom and dad, with love.

Special thanks to Deborah Balmuth, Lisa Hiley, and Melinda Sheehan for your guidance in making this book the best it could be.

CONTENTS

....

INTRODUCTION

....

Parenting is one of the hardest tasks any person can undertake and one for which most of us feel the least prepared. First-time parents can easily feel overwhelmed with the never-ending responsibilities that accompany the arrival of a newborn. Even experienced parents encounter moments of exasperation and desperation. But while parents are busy with the basics of caring for a baby, it's important for them to remember that their precious little one won't be little for long and that each step of the way represents a window of opportunity for growth. Even (perhaps especially) the ordinary events that make up a regular day are part of the process.

Pampering a baby comes naturally — a kiss, a hug, or a few whispered words of tenderness flow easily from a loving parent. But in addition to these endearing expressions of affection, there are many more ways in which parents can positively impact the spirit and well-being of a developing child. And they can do so in ways that are in accord with the principles of natural living and simply having fun.

This book is not about raising a child. There are volumes of books that will help you bear up through the difficulties of sibling rivalry, the traumas of childhood diseases, and the complexities of toilet training. This book offers various simple and common sense ways to nurture your child in the first year of life to provide the best foundation for wellness, self-esteem, and a lasting parental bond. The benefits that you both reap will endure a lifetime and become instilled in future generations.

As a parent, you naturally want the best for your baby. But the best gift you can give your child isn't a college education or annual vacations to Disneyland; it's the gift of yourself. This book will help you impart that gift freely in ways that may be new to you or in ways that you may never have considered.

Parenting is an adventure! Like a spin on the Ferris wheel, this lifelong commitment will be filled with highs and lows. Enjoy the all-too-short ride.

Information and Cautions

All of the ingredients used in the formulas throughout this book can be found in health food stores, in some supermarkets, and through online suppliers. See Resources to help you locate and obtain various supplies and equipment.

Always measure all ingredients carefully and keep them stored away from children and pets. Essential oils are highly concentrated and should always be handled with particular caution. Do not use essential oils undiluted unless specified or in amounts greater than recommended, and never use them internally.

Should any rash, redness, or other skin irritation develop after using any formula or ingredient, discontinue its use and seek the advice of a qualified health care practitioner.

Babies are such a nice way to start people.

— Don Herald

CHAPTER 1

NEST BUILDING 101

....

Just as you would avoid feeding your baby harmful substances, you also want to limit her exposure to environmental toxins. Furniture, paints, and other materials can emit potentially harmful chemicals without you even knowing it. In fact, the pollutant level inside the average home is much greater than that of the outdoors! By using nontoxic materials, you can make the nursery a safe place as well as a cozy haven.

....

*Children are likely to live up
to what you believe of them.*

— Lady Bird Johnson

THE NATURAL NURSERY

....

Dress your baby in organic fabrics made from natural cotton, hemp, wool, or linen (flax). Natural clothing is soft, free of toxic chemicals and dyes, and available in beautiful, lush earth tones. Organic clothing is also better for the environment. Natural fleece, for instance, is often made from recycled plastic bottles without generating any production waste. Organic wool clothing is produced without the use of pesticides. Even soy and bamboo are being used to produce natural clothing these days.

Aside from providing superior comfort and durability, these materials are a renewable source and readily biodegrade. Look for the 'Certified Organic' designation on the label, which indicates that the product has received third-party verification that it has been manufactured according to organic standards.

The bedding you choose for your baby's crib is important. Look for bumpers, mattress pads, and pillows (for older babies) made of and filled with cotton; not only are they softer and more comfortable than synthetic items, but they're also more durable and free of chemical residues. In addition, natural fibers allow air to circulate better through the material and they resist trapping odors. A mattress made of organic materials is a good idea also.

Wrap your baby in an all-natural blanket. Several companies make baby blankets of 100 percent organic cotton or bamboo-combed fleece (80 percent bamboo fibers and 20 percent cotton). They last for years and provide soft comfort without the use of synthetic fibers or cotton grown with pesticides.

Garage sales and auctions are great places to find unusual pieces of furniture for the nursery. But if you invest in used furniture or use hand-me-downs, you'll need to check all parts and hardware for wear that could cause injury. You might also want to remove the finish and use a natural paint or stain and a nontoxic sealant.

A futon in the nursery? Sure! Futons aren't just for adults anymore. Several companies manufacture crib futons made from all-natural, nontoxic materials. For newborns, "Moses-style" woven baskets provide an alternative to traditional bassinets.

DREAMY DECOR

....

Create a dreamy wall or ceiling mural with clouds, stars, suns, and moons! Such fantasy works of art will not only soothe and entertain your baby, but also spark his creative imagination.

Think of a theme. Forego the typical blue for boys and pink for girls motif and deck out the nursery with a unisex theme and color scheme. How about a jungle room, complete with a pack of wild (stuffed) animals lying about and walls painted or wallpapered to look like a rainforest? Or create a fantasy garden with vines and vibrantly colored flowers climbing a trellis.

TERRIFIC TIP

Distract baby during diaper changes. Place a brightly colored mobile above the changing table and she'll be less likely to squirm around. Or give her a chunky book or small toy that she can hold on to instead of grabbing at the diaper wipes.

Color your baby's world with natural paints, pigments, and stains. Nearly 10 percent of airborne pollutants in the home come from volatile organic compounds (VOCs) in paint. Many of the larger paint manufacturers now produce low-VOC paints, and several companies produce natural paint alternatives, such as casein paint, which is derived from milk, in a variety of rich colors.

Casein paint is not only VOC free but is the oldest and most durable form of paint available. In fact, milk paint has been found on decorative pieces buried in King Tut's tomb!

NONTOXIC, DO-IT-YOURSELF PAINT

....

This paint spreads easily and imparts rich color while allowing wood to breathe. Use it on wood furniture, doors, moldings, and window frames. You can also use this paint on dry wall or other absorbent surfaces.

    3 cups turpentine (this ingredient is made
        from pine resin and is nontoxic)

    1 cup linseed oil

    5–6 tablespoons mineral pigment

    2 tablespoons drying agent

Mix all ingredients together until well blended. With a soft cloth or a natural-bristle brush, apply paint to the prepared wall or wood surface and allow to penetrate for 30 minutes. Wipe off excess.

For deeper color, repeat these steps as many times as you wish. When the paint is completely dry, coat the surface with a nontoxic sealant if desired.

Cleanup: Fill a glass jar with a few inches of turpentine and a few drops of natural dish liquid or liquid castile soap. Leave the brush to soak for 20 minutes, then rinse it clean with warm water.

Storage: Keep leftover paint in a glass jar with a tight fitting screw top. As long as air doesn't get into the jar, the mixture can be stored for up to six months. Remember to label the container and give the solution a thorough stirring before using again.

Look for other earth-friendly products and accessories that you can use to reduce toxicity in the home, such as natural flooring and carpeting made from recycled plastic bottles. See Resources for ideas and sources.

INTO THE MOUTHS
OF BABES

....

Recent reports have warned that certain materials used in making baby bottles, teethers, and soft plastic toys, especially those designed to make their way to a baby's mouth, may present risks to children. Of primary concern is polyvinyl chloride (PVC), otherwise known as vinyl, as well as a phthalate dubbed DINP. These chemicals can be absorbed from certain teethers and toys and have even been found to leach into infant formula from plastic bottles. Studies have linked these agents to liver damage and cancer. To be sure your baby is completely safe, you'll want to avoid these materials.

Replace shiny "plastic" bottles (their packaging does not always specify what they're actually made of) with glass bottles or those made from a dull, opaque plastic. The latter are often colored and made from polyethylene and do not leach bisphenol A (BPA), another questionable component.

BUY WISELY

....

Manufacturers are not required to disclose the inclusion of phthalates in their products. However, products containing artificial fragrances and synthetic chemicals are more likely to have them, so be sure to read labels carefully. In addition, avoid bottles and toys that have the recycling codes 3 (PVC) and 7 (polycarbonate), which are more likely to contain phthalates, chlorine, and other toxins.

Opt for toys made from wood or cloth instead of plastic. The Internet is a wonderful source for craftspeople and hobbyists who make and sell old-fashioned wooden and fabric toys. You'll also find

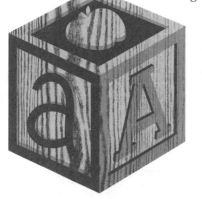

listings for companies offering natural baby products, including toys and stuffed animals made without dyes or other irritants.

MAKE-YOUR-OWN PLAYTHINGS

....

Safe and creative playthings for baby can be quickly assembled from ordinary household items. Plastic bowls and wooden spoons from the kitchen will inspire your little drummer. Older babies will enjoy stacking various sized bowls and cups. Other toys that may be lurking in your kitchen or pantry include:

- Measuring cups and spoons

- A cupcake tin and some small items to sort

- Rubber spatulas

- Tea towels (great for playing peek-a-boo and making other objects disappear)

- Plastic containers with lids that can stack on top of each other

PVC-free plastic cups, bottles, or bowls can entertain and teach at bath time too. Baby will enjoy filling such items with water and spilling the water out again. This activity is especially fun if you poke a hole or two in the bottom of some of the playthings.

Make sponges into fun blocks for bath time. Just cut them into interesting shapes with a sharp knife or scissors and toss them into the tub to float. Show baby how to have fun stacking or squeezing the water from them. Soon he'll learn that pushing the sponge block down into the water results in a surprising pop up when he lets go!

I will make you brooches and toys
for your delight
Of birdsong at morning and
starshine at night.

— Robert Louis Stevenson

MAKE YOUR HOME CLEAN AND GREEN

....

Visit your local health food store to learn about organic, nontoxic products for garden, pets, and laundry. Commercial laundry products may contain toxic ingredients that can leave a residue on clothing, and home and garden pesticides are associated with an increased risk of brain cancer and leukemia in children. Even the most ordinary household cleaning products may pose a threat if handled improperly or accidentally swallowed.

Always store your natural cleaners and the ingredients used to make them away from children and pets. Just because they are organic and nontoxic doesn't mean that they cannot still cause illness, skin irritation, or allergic reaction if handled or swallowed.

TERRIFIC TIP

For a natural spray disinfectant,
fill a 22-ounce spray bottle with
1 cup of vinegar, 1 cup of water, and
15 drops each of thyme, rosemary,
and tea tree essential oils. Keep a bottle
in the bathroom and one near your
main diaper-changing area. Stash a
travel size bottle in your diaper bag
and/or glove compartment for
quick cleanups.

Being a mother enables one to influence the future.

— Jane Sellman

CHAPTER 2

BRINGING BABY HOME

CHAPTER 2

Whether or not you launched a career before taking on the role of parent, you can expect that your new occupation will be equally demanding on a full-time scale. In fact, it's been said that all mothers are working mothers, and that includes those who choose not to return to their previous professions. In addition to the decision to work outside the home, you will need to address a number of other issues as well, such as making informed decisions about nursing, circumcision, and the diapering method that best suits your lifestyle.

*I looked on child rearing not
only as a work of love and duty but
as a profession that was fully
as interesting and challenging as any
honorable profession in the world
and one that demanded the best I
could bring to it.*

—Rose Kennedy

NURSING IS GOOD FOR BOTH OF YOU

There's no doubt that breast milk is the perfect food for your baby. Nursing fosters a close bond between mother and child and helps reduce your baby's risk of allergies, asthma, and a host of diseases. Nursing also offers extra benefits for mom. It burns calories and helps the uterus return to its normal size after labor.

The earlier you start, the better. Ideally, you should first nurse your newborn within an hour after delivery, when the sucking instinct is quite strong. At this early stage, your breasts won't be producing milk but rather a fluid called colostrum that contains protective antibodies.

TIPS FOR NURSING

....

Choose a quiet, restful place. The more at ease you are when nursing, the more successful both you and baby will be.

Nurse on demand. And newborns do demand to be fed often, about every two hours. Don't worry, you won't run out of milk! In fact, the more often you nurse, the more milk you'll produce.

Find the right position. Proper positioning helps reduce soreness for mom and makes less work for baby. Make sure you place the nipple as far back in the baby's mouth as possible.

Try to avoid in-between snacks. Supplementing a nursing baby with formula may spoil his appetite for mother's milk. If your baby seems hungry and you're too exhausted to nurse again, have someone give him a bottle of expressed milk.

Believe it or not, a baby's jaw has three times the strength of an adult's!

OUCH! WHAT TO DO FOR SWOLLEN BREASTS

....

Engorgement of the breasts is common in the first few days after birth. You'll find relief by — you guessed it — nursing your baby. Or you can relieve the discomfort with warm baths and compresses.

While breast-feeding may be natural, it isn't a given that everything will go smoothly. Both you and your baby are learning a new skill; if you don't feel that you're both on the same page, your midwife, physician, or local Le Leche League representative can help you.

GO WITH THE FLOW

....

When you first begin nursing your baby, you will quickly learn that your milk flow seems to magically turn "on" whenever your baby cries from hunger. This is known as the "letdown reflex," and it's a perfectly normal and desirable response. It's interesting that this reaction usually occurs only when your own baby cries and not in response to another.

While this built-in mechanism ensures that your baby's needs are met, it can lead to embarrassing moments for you. Plan to wear plenty of old sweatshirts and flannel shirts until you and your baby become more in sync with a regular feeding schedule. Special pads or even ordinary cotton cloths tucked into a nursing bra can help to absorb any leakage.

GUILT-FREE
BOTTLE-FEEDING

There are scores of reasons why a new mother might elect to bottle-feed rather than breast-feed, every one of them valid. It's ironic that breast-feeding (especially in public) was once considered "radical." Today, the tables have turned, and a mother can sometimes feel guilty or inadequate for not nursing her baby. But most doctors agree that bottle-feeding is a perfectly adequate substitute for breast-feeding. If going back to work is the issue, you can collect breast milk with a breast pump and store it in the refrigerator or freezer. This allows fathers and caregivers to feed the baby as well.

The important thing to remember is that how you feed your baby is entirely your decision and that you must do what is comfortable for you and your lifestyle.

Try not to imagine that you're being given sideways glances of disapproval. Have faith in the old adage that "mother knows best."

And keep in mind that formula-fed babies thrive just as well as breast-fed babies. In fact, you might have been fed from a bottle — and you turned out great!

FORMULA FOR SUCCESS

....

Is the combination route right for you? Many new mothers choose to start out breast-feeding and then switch to formula soon after birth. This offers the benefit of giving your baby the antibodies he needs right at the beginning before you start adapting him to the bottle. When it's time, most babies will accept the "other" nipple just as readily as they do your own.

Some moms also find that they can successfully nurse two or three times a day and have someone else (dad or a childcare provider) give bottles at the other feedings. If you encounter any transitional problems, consult your doctor or midwife for advice.

Nurturing a baby is not centered solely around the breast. If it were, fathers would be left out in the cold! Rest assured that there are many other ways for you to nurture your infant. Nursing offers a natural way to bond and feel close, but so does bottle-feeding — along with bathing, playing, and snuggling.

Never grab a bottle straight from the refrigerator and give it to your baby. Since breast milk is always served at just the right temperature, it's reasonable to assume that formula should be too. Cold liquids can cause gastrointestinal distress for an infant.

So let the formula come to room temperature or warm it slightly in the microwave (loosen the cap first!) for 20 to 30 seconds. If you do this, always shake the bottle and then test the formula on the inside of your wrist to make sure it isn't too hot for your baby — body temperature is what you're aiming for.

Note: Be sure you're using a microwave-safe bottle.

COMMON REASONS FOR BOTTLE-FEEDING

....

There are many good reasons why a mother may choose to bottle-feed instead of breast-feed. The following are a few of them:

- Returning to work

- Mother is ill or on medication

- Difficulty in establishing breast-feeding

- Adoption

- Breast disease

- Periods of separation from baby

- Medical complications from nursing

- Baby's sensitivity to mother's diet

TAKE CARE OF YOURSELF

....

It's important to take care of yourself and keep up your strength while you are adjusting to your new routine. Don't forget that your hormones are hopping in the weeks and even months after giving birth. Make sure that you get enough rest, eat right, and take a few moments each day to ground and center by taking a brief walk, listening to some soothing music, reading for a few minutes, or doing something that is just for you.

LET OTHERS TAKE CARE OF YOU

....

Your family and friends will want to help — let them. Accept offers to prepare meals or run errands. Let someone else mow the lawn, walk the dog, do laundry, and even take your car in for servicing if that's what you need. Ask a grandparent or a special friend to pay extra attention to siblings.

BOTTOMS UP!

....

What goes in baby also comes out, several times a day. So, where do all those dirty diapers go? The answer is the landfill, to the tune of 50 million every day, or more than 18 billion per year, according to the Environmental Protection Agency (EPA). What's worse is, that's where they'll stay for about five centuries. (Yes, you read that right!)

TERRIFIC TIP

Make diapering time easier by having everything you need to do the job within your reach — but out of baby's. Also, always keep one hand on your baby while changing him, since squirming and kicking can quickly land your budding gymnast on the floor.

THE GREAT DIAPER DEBATE

Just a few years ago, the debate over whether to use cloth or disposable diapers could have only been settled by deciding to either endure a stinky diaper pail or risk compromising the hygiene of the environment. Today, however, there are choices available that make both options easier to live with.

Chlorine-free disposable diapers have been on the market for some time now. The absence of chlorine reduces the amount of dioxin, a known carcinogen, from being released into the environment as a by-product of chlorine degradation. The diaper material itself is made of wood pulp (known as "fluff") and polyolefin fabric and film as opposed to petroleum-based materials. However, while this is a better alternative to conventional diapers, the problem of the plastic portion of the diaper ending up in the landfill may still exist. Unless the polyolefin fibers have been treated with an accelerant to promote the chemical breakdown of the plastic by microorganisms in the environment, they do not readily biodegrade. If in doubt, check with the manufacturer.

Cloth diapers remove the problem of creating toxic waste, unless you consider the fact that they may end up soaking in a diaper pail for a week or more before you have a chance to launder them. If you've ever stuck your nose in one, then you know how pungent the odor can be. Of course, advances have been made in this department as well and odor-controlling diaper pails are now available.

However, cloth diapers may pose a potential risk for diaper rash to develop since the cloth doesn't pull wetness away from baby's skin as gel-enhanced conventional diapers do. Also, there's the concern over additional energy and fuel being expended to launder them. On the plus side, cloth diapers make the best dusting cloths ever conceived.

Ready for a refreshing change? There's a new kind of diaper in town — gDiapers. These diapers are also chlorine free and made of natural wood pulp fibers, but are 100 percent biodegradable. In fact, they're designed to flush down the toilet.

According to the manufacturer, you can even compost the diapers (wet ones only), which will biodegrade in 50 to 150 days. Go to the Web site to watch a brief movie that shows a gDiaper completely biodegrading in 60 days while its conventional disposable cousin reposes next to it intact.

Diaper backward spells repaid.
Think about it.

— Marshall McLuhan

WHY NOT DITCH THE DIAPER ALTOGETHER?

....

There's a new movement (pardon the pun) among parents today: Forgoing diapers in favor of starting potty training from birth. The concept has long been practiced in rural areas around the globe, where diapers are in short supply or parents simply can't afford them. However, in the West, this old method of toilet training has now been given several technical names, including Elimination Communication (or simply EC), Natural Infant Hygiene, Infant Potty Training, and even Potty Whispering. Whatever you choose to call it, the method is quickly gaining in popularity.

The idea behind diaperless toilet training has three parts: Learning to recognize baby's signal of the need to go potty, offering cue sounds that mimic the act, and providing positive places to associate with going to the bathroom. In practice, mom picks up on the body language of her baby that indicates a call of nature, which may be a squeezed fist or a certain wiggle-dance. She then takes her child to the loo and holds her in place while making a "whizzing" sound. Hopefully, the act is completed and goes down the drain. (Although one has to wonder what kind of sound to make to mimic a bowel movement.)

There are some obvious and some not-so-obvious pros and cons to the EC method. For one thing, not buying diapers is environmentally friendly, not to mention easier on the family budget. It also eliminates the need for toting heavy diaper bags everywhere, as well as the risk of diaper rash.

The method may raise a few eyebrows in public restrooms, not to mention the reaction at grandma's house. How many accidents occur on the couch before achieving success? And where on earth does one find infant-sized underwear? Clearly, going this unconventional route isn't for the thin-skinned. Still, if you'd like to learn more about this method of toilet training, visit *www.diaperfreebaby.org*.

CIRCUMCISION: THE CHOICE ISN'T ALWAYS CLEAR-CUT

....

More than 85 percent of the male population on the planet passes through childhood with all of their original parts, including the foreskin (technically known as the "prepuce") that surrounds the tip of the penis. While the number of circumcisions routinely performed in the western world has dropped considerably in the last 25 years, about 60 percent of male newborns are still circumcised in the United States.

Contrary to popular belief, circumcision is not an artifact of modern society. In fact, the procedure was commonly practiced in ancient Egypt and Africa and may be one of the oldest surgeries known to man. In addition, circumcision has religious significance in various cultures throughout history and the world.

ARGUMENTS FOR CIRCUMCISION

....

- Social acceptance, self-esteem, and body image. Some boys may worry about being physically different from their peers and may suffer teasing from other boys in gym class, locker rooms, and so on.

- Reduced risk of urinary tract infections. On average, a circumcised male has a 1 in 1,000 chance of contracting a urinary tract infection compared to 1 in 100 for an uncircumcised male.

- Reduced risk of penile cancer. While incidence is rare, circumcision in infancy provides 100 percent protection from cancer of the penis.

- Eliminated risk of balanitis, a condition characterized by chronic inflammation of the glans.

- Circumcised men are eight times less likely to develop HIV or AIDS.

- Reduced risk of transmitting the human papilloma virus, which can flourish in the foreskin and cause cervical cancer in women.

ARGUMENTS AGAINST CIRCUMCISION

....

- With rare exceptions, there is no medical reason to remove the foreskin.

- It is reasonable to assume that the procedure is painful. (Fortunately, at least, the American Academy of Pediatrics now recommends some form of anesthesia, which wasn't the case for many years.)

- Circumcision can lead in rare cases to complications, such as infection, excessive bleeding, or permanent injury to the penis.

- Narrowing of the urethra sometimes occurs after circumcision, and may require further surgery.

- Studies have shown that circumcised male children have a stronger reaction to pain associated with childhood vaccinations, especially those who didn't receive anesthesia prior to circumcision.

- Studies have shown that proper hygiene instruction will also effectively reduce the risk for contracting or spreading disease or infection.

- Some men, particularly those circumcised later in life, insist that the removal of the foreskin reduces physical sensation.

RETURNING TO WORK

....

Most parents struggle to meet the demands of home, children, and a career. Even if you work from home, or make child rearing your main job, sooner or later another caregiver will come into the picture. In fact, nearly 70 percent of parents with young children place them in some kind of daily care situation. Before hiring outside help, arm yourself with a few common sense guidelines for finding appropriate and responsible care for your child.

TERRIFIC TIP

Whether your childcare arrangements
are in-home or away from home,
exercise your right to an open-door
policy. Make occasional surprise
visits to observe what's going on
when you're not present.

HELP WANTED

....

If you are returning to work soon after having your baby, you may choose to have someone care for your child in your own home. A relative might be the best choice, but a trusted friend or neighbor can become part of your child's extended family as well. You can also ask friends and neighbors for recommendations for a childcare provider.

If you're hiring a nanny or au pair, hire one through a reputable agency that can conduct a thorough background check, including a criminal record investigation. According to the International Nanny Association, about 5 percent of nannies applying for a job have criminal convictions. Most of these are attracted to newspaper ads and agencies that will not check their backgrounds.

Thoroughly interview your caregiving candidates at least twice. Here are some topics to bring up:

- Why do they want to work with young children?

- Do they share your attitudes about child rearing?

- Why did their last job end?

- Play the "What if" game and ask how they would handle specific situations.

- Follow through by contacting references.

If you are considering a childcare center for your baby, talk with other parents whose children have attended or currently attend the center. Find out the ratio of caregivers to children and how the center handles different age groups. Discuss the center's policies toward illness, emergency closings, and other important issues so you know what to expect when a situation arises. Visit a couple of times before making your decision.

A childcare home, where a primary adult provides care in his or her own home, is another option. Interview and spend some time with the adult in charge. Is the home licensed and regularly inspected? How many children will this person be caring for each day? Will your child receive the attention appropriate for her age?

In any childcare situation, trust your gut. If any red flags about your care provider surface, or if your child begins to respond negatively to a care provider, you need to reevaluate the situation and make changes accordingly.

BELIEVE IN YOURSELF

....

Confidence makes for better parents — and better babies. But sometimes, especially for first-time parents, it can be daunting to imagine being completely responsible for such a fragile bundle of joy. Whenever those thoughts of "Can I really do this?" begin to surface, close your eyes and say one of the affirmations on the next page to yourself... or say them out loud for the world to hear!

It wouldn't hurt to make the recitation of self-validating affirmations part of a daily ritual. It won't be long before automatic negative thoughts become positive ones and you discover that your inner voice has better things to say about you.

POSITIVE AFFIRMATIONS FOR PARENTS

....

- I am a capable and loving parent. My thoughts, words, and actions reflect this every day.

- My instincts are worth trusting.

- I am my baby's teacher. But, most of what I need to know I will learn from my baby.

- I can choose to take or not take advice when it's offered.

- Every moment isn't perfect, but I'll miss the ones that matter if I stay "in my head," thinking about what I "should" have done.

- There are many challenges ahead, but I am ready to face them with confidence, ability, and humor.

DISCIPLINE BEGINS IN INFANCY

....

If the idea of disciplining a small creature still attached to a diaper seems over the top to you, then perhaps you need to reevaluate what discipline means to you. The American Academy of Pediatrics identifies the main disciplinary objective of parents as providing a structured routine, as well as being responsive to an infant's needs.

But consider for a moment that the word "disciple," which literally means student or follower, is at the root of the word "discipline." On a basic level, then, it would be more accurate to say that exercising discipline simply means to teach and guide, without punishment.

Mothers have been instinctively disciplining their children from the first day of life since the beginning of time. Young babies are redirected when a hazardous object travels to their mouth. Older babies are taught by example what behavior is socially acceptable. Child rearing is all about setting boundaries so that our children may learn self-control and governance when we're not around.

COMMUNICATION IS KEY

....

Someday — you can plan on it — your baby will become one of those little understood and sometimes even less tolerated human beings known as teenagers. A fair amount of rebellion is expected at that time, but you may experience considerably less if you establish healthy and honest communication from the start.

For instance, responding to an infant's cry does not spoil the child; it promotes communication. Your child will learn to feel secure because your readiness establishes a strong bond and trust between you.

Sometime before her first birthday your child will master the word "no." She will not only comprehend its meaning, but she will also learn to use this word to get a rise out of you. In other words, she will begin to test limits. This is not flawed behavior. It's a display of developing independence and a sign that she feels secure enough to risk your displeasure.

In motherhood, there's so much to learn, so much to give, and although the learning gets less with each succeeding child, the giving never does.

— Marguerite Kelly

CHAPTER 3

THE ART
OF
ATTACHMENT

Two of the most important gifts you will ever give your child are a feeling of security and the knowledge that he is worthy of unconditional love. Bonding truly begins at birth and it continues to grow with each passing year. How you bond with your baby, and how soon, will impact his well-being in a way that will last a lifetime.

Unfortunately, babies don't come into the world with blueprints or an owner's manual. But, incredibly, your baby does come equipped with built-in mechanisms to tell you when something is wrong or when everything is right with his world — signals generally recognized as crying and cooing.

In the sheltered simplicity of the first days after a baby is born, one sees again the magical closed circle, the miraculous sense of two people existing only for each other.

— Anne Morrow Lindbergh

"IN ME I TRUST!"

....

It may seem to you that everyone else seems to know what's best for your baby, even better than you do. People love to give advice when it comes to a complicated "device" such as an infant. But sometimes too much information can leave you feeling inept, as though you're doing everything wrong. How can you keep your sanity during these times? By trusting yourself.

TERRIFIC TIP

When bottle-feeding, switch baby to
your other arm halfway through the
meal. This will help to relieve stress
on your neck and shoulders. It will
also offer baby the chance to enjoy a
different view of his surroundings,
something that occurs naturally
when shifting sides during
breast-feeding.

THE TIES THAT BIND

························

Stay connected. If you haven't yet delivered, ask your obstetrician or midwife to delay severing the umbilical cord for as long as possible (usually about 15 minutes). There are several good reasons for this. For instance, researchers at the University of California have found that delaying cutting (or even clamping) the umbilical cord significantly increases an infant's available iron reserves for several months. For premature babies, delayed cutting reduces the risk of bleeding in the brain and the need for transfusions.

PRECIOUS MOMENTS

....

The first moments and days after baby's birth are precious indeed. Try to keep your baby in your hospital room or bedroom instead of the nursery as much as possible. You have a lot to learn about each other.

Look for signs of success. During the first month of life, an infant's main goal is to become in sync with his environment. From two to six months, however, baby's rhythm shifts to becoming "as one" with his parents. Longer periods of eye contact, smiling, cooing, and careful study of your facial features are all signs of positive attachment.

Make faces at baby. By the age of two months, an infant can distinguish between pictures of faces with misplaced features and those with the eyes, nose, and mouth in the right place. That's because she's been busy studying your face all this time. Babies also enjoy variations in facial expressions, so let your face be the canvas from which she can draw from. In another month or so, she'll be the one initiating facial gestures for you to mimic.

WHAT'S IN A NAME?

....

In addition to your own favorite choices and family traditions, there are many good books that can help you select an appropriate name for your baby. Choose carefully — it's an imprint that will last for life. You can even hold your own naming ceremony to celebrate your new arrival.

Enjoy your baby's smile. It's intoxicating — literally. Research shows that moms actually get a buzz from seeing their baby smile. This reaction is evidenced by brain scans revealing that certain areas of the brain light up, the same ones associated with other pleasurable experiences that result in an increase of dopamine release, such as sex or savoring a piece of chocolate.

Let your cup overflow. Cuddling your baby is a healthy way of nurturing him both emotionally and physically. Pooh-pooh anyone who tries to convince you that you'll spoil your baby if you pick him up too often.

Establish a network with other new parents. The couples you met during childbirth classes are the very folks going through the same trials as you; just sharing your day-to-day joys and concerns can be enough to get you through the rough spots.

DON'T CRY OVER
SPILT MILK

....

Accept the fact that you'll make mistakes in the beginning. If you feel you can't yet flawlessly change a diaper or burp a baby, rest assured that you'll get better in time. Practice, after all, makes perfect.

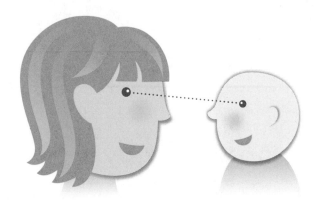

Keep the apple in your eye. **In the early days, your baby will not be able to focus and will have her eyes closed much of the time. But expressing your love for her through voice and touch will comfort and soothe her.**

Keep your eye on the apple. **When your baby is able to better focus on your face, encourage frequent periods of eye contact. Such sessions help establish a loving and trustful bond. Always include touch when looking into your baby's eyes; stroke her head, face, or hands.**

My mom is a never-ending song in my heart of comfort, happiness, and being. I may sometimes forget the words but I always remember the tune.

— Graycie Harmon

Don't even think about trying to do it all! For the first several weeks, babies have their own ideas about when they should eat and sleep — and if you try to make your baby adapt to your schedule, you might find yourself forgetting simple things, like your social security number, your sister's name, or where you keep the washing machine.

When baby is resting, you should be, too. Believe me, the dirt on the kitchen floor will still be there later. (And don't let other people's negative opinions of your housekeeping get under your skin!)

SLING YOUR BABY

....

The over-the-shoulder baby holder is an ancient device that plays an important role in "attachment" parenting — a philosophy of maintaining maximum physical closeness as well as responsiveness and sensitivity to baby's needs. Research shows that regular "baby wearing" reduces daytime crying by 43 percent and nighttime crying by 51 percent. In addition, babies frequently carried in a sling spend more time in a "quiet-alert state," which promotes learning, coping ability, and bonding with parents. Choose a sling made of good quality organic cotton or hemp.

There's nothing like the feel of that small warm body next to your own. Snuggle with your baby often — while she's sleeping or nursing, or just when you both would enjoy a few moments alone together.

TERRIFIC TIP

Newborns have underdeveloped immune systems and can easily catch a cold from a well-meaning friend or relative. Try to limit visitors to immediate family for the first few weeks. There will be plenty of time to introduce the rest of the world to your baby later on.

MUSIC TO LITTLE EARS

....

Give your developing baby the gift of music. Babies don't really prefer one style of music over another. So, if you find jazz or rock and roll more soothing than classical, play on!

Sing to your baby while walking, working around the house, or just sitting quietly. I sang the same song every day during my pregnancy and then for years after as a lullaby.

Attend a musical event. If you enjoy concerts and recitals, introduce them to baby now! You'll both find the music stimulating and relaxing. Just make sure it's a baby-friendly venue, and sit near an exit in case your baby becomes *too* stimulated.

Promote bonding through laughter. About a month after baby's first smile appears, she may suddenly emit a giggle in response to an object or event. However, she's not necessarily laughing because she finds something amusing. In fact, babies sometimes laugh when they are startled or confused over an event or object as a precursor to crying.

You can help baby to learn to feel more at ease with her environment by encouraging her to laugh more. Playing "piggy" with her toes or making silly faces at the right moment can turn a potentially upsetting experience into an opportunity to form a greater bond and mutual trust. She'll also learn that her actions can have a positive effect on you.

Read some of your favorite poems or stories out
loud. If you have other children, invite them to read
along with you, or ask them to read to the baby.

Go for a swim. Newborns take to water naturally. After all, they spent nine months immersed! Whether it's in your backyard pool or the community pool at the YMCA, your baby will find floating in water very soothing.

Skip the water wings, though; they can slip off or tangle on little arms. Instead, look for a swim vest that allows even the smallest of babies to safely float on their backs. You can use it in the tub too! Supervision is required.

RUB-A-DUB-DUB, FUN IN THE TUB

Bath time should be fun for both parent and baby! Just make sure the room is warm and free of drafts, and gather everything you'll need before you get started. Here are some tips for a splashing good time:

Instead of using a terry washcloth, invest in a large cellulose sponge. They're soft and squishy (adding to the fun value), and they last a long time.

A soft, 100 percent cotton hooded towel is great for wrapping up baby when the splishing and splashing is over. It's a perfect way to keep baby warm and cozy while you snuggle up for a story, to nurse, or to take a nap together.

Talk, sing, or recite poetry to your baby while bathing her. Even if no one else appreciates your oratory talents, your baby will be captivated by the rhythm of your voice, especially when it's combined with your soothing touch.

Take a bath with your baby when she's older than three months. Just make sure the water temperature is adjusted for baby's tender skin, not yours, and take care to keep her head above water level.

DIFFERENT STROKES FOR LITTLE FOLKS

....

Massage is relaxing and comforting for both parent and baby. It offers healthful benefits by improving circulation, helping digestion, and providing a sense of well-being. Also, touch is an excellent way to bond with your little one.

TERRIFIC TIP

If your baby fusses during a massage, take that as her cue that the session is over for now. She may be chilly, hungry, or just not in the mood.

THE BASICS OF INFANT MASSAGE

Most babies love having their chest and back rubbed. But avoid doing so when baby has a full tummy or is hungry.

- Massage is very soothing, especially if used in combination with a story or song. It doesn't have to be anything fancy — a constant circular motion on the back or belly will do. You can also gently stroke your baby's face or massage her hands. Make sure the room in which you're giving the massage is warm and free of drafts.

- Always put the massage oil on your hands first and rub them together a few times to warm the oil. The perfect oil to use is plain sweet almond oil.

- Remove baby's clothing — but you might want to keep the diaper in place, especially if your lovely baby is a boy. Otherwise, you might be in for an unpleasant surprise. Also, remove any jewelry before giving a massage to reduce the risk of injury or irritation.

- Always ask permission to massage before you begin, even if baby is too young to understand your request or to offer a response. This will help to instill a sense of body ownership and healthy touch when your child is older.

- To massage the head and face, use small circular motions with your fingertips around the forehead, brow line, temples, and jaw line. Try to maintain a hand-over-hand action so that one hand is always in motion during the massage. Do not massage near the eyes or the fontanel (soft spot on top of the head).

- When massaging arms and legs, simple downward strokes are effective. Don't forget about those tiny fingers and feet!

LIFE WITH BABY, SIBLINGS, AND PETS

....

Imagine how you would feel if your spouse came home with another companion to live with you both, without even consulting you first. Well, that's probably how a toddler or a beloved pet feels when you bring a new baby into the house. It's important to take their feelings into consideration so that you can nurture a happy and healthy relationship between your baby and other family members.

A TIME FOR EVERYONE

....

What does a baby demand most from you? Your time. And that's exactly what siblings and pets are going to miss having with you. Carve out some time each day to spend with your other children or to play with your pets to remind them that they're special.

Get older siblings in on the act. Let them help you with caring for and playing with your new baby. A big brother or sister can be a true help by entertaining the baby during diaper changes or bringing you items while you're nursing or have your hands full. But be extra alert: A toddler has no idea how much stronger he is than his baby sister; he cannot "put on the brakes" and may cause harm if unsupervised.

MEET THE PETS

....

Ideally, dogs and cats should already have plenty of people experience before they're introduced to a new baby. For that matter, the best way to introduce your pet to a new baby is to start before she's born. Let pets inspect the baby's room. The more you try to keep them away, the more they'll want to check out the baby after she arrives. They may even perceive the "shoo" treatment as a sign that the baby is a threat.

Show baby how to properly touch your pet. Nobody likes to have his ears and tail pulled! Also teach your baby that fingers, hands, and articles of clothing are not playthings for your pet.

Always supervise your pet and baby when they're together, but let them interact. With proper handling, your pet will become a longtime, cherished companion for your baby.

Raise a happy baby by allowing him to be unhappy at appropriate times. During the first six months of life, it's important that you respond to your child's immediate needs. But as baby learns to sit, crawl, and reach for objects, he needs to learn how to cope with a certain level of discomfort in order to experience success. So don't be afraid to let baby fuss a bit or refrain from running over to him the instant he drops his favorite toy. Give him a few moments to try to work out a solution by himself.

Keep baby happy while you're busy with necessary tasks. Running errands or doing basic household chores while caring for a baby can be challenging. Some babies enjoy the change of scenery that comes with being strapped into a car seat or grocery cart; others may resent the disruption in their normal routine.

At home, try to do dishes or vacuum during baby's naptime. Combine folding the laundry with one-on-one playtime with your baby — both activities can occupy the same clean floor space. If you find your baby becoming fussy as you stand in line at the grocery store, make up a song or rhyme about some of the items in your cart to engage him. If nothing else, your fellow shoppers will be entertained.

NIGHTY-NIGHT

·····················

Establishing a regular bedtime routine will benefit the whole family. Start with a soothing herbal bath and then perhaps a snuggling or nursing session. Rocking is another calming activity. The last step of the routine, from a favorite story to a poem or lullaby, should always take place in the baby's crib or bed.

Purchase lullaby tapes to play softly in the background to help baby slip off to sleep by herself. Look for instrumental melodies, a lilting human voice, or even a rhythmic heartbeat.

Sleep, my child, and peace attend thee
All through the night.
Guardian angels God will send thee,
All through the night.
Soft the drowsy hours are creeping
Hill and vale in slumber sleeping.
I my loving vigil keeping,
All through the night.

— Traditional Welsh lullaby

Help your baby learn the difference between night and day. While your home should be a stimulating place for baby during the day, it should be peaceful and quiet at night.

Try to limit visitors and curb any noisy activities in the evening. This will help baby to establish his own circadian rhythm that coincides with your household.

MOTHER'S MILK TEA

....

It's hard to sooth and nurture a fussy baby when you're feeling tired and stressed. Here's a formula for soothing and nurturing yourself before you sit down to rock a cranky baby. It has the added advantage of helping your milk to flow more easily.

1 ounce dried chamomile flowers

1 ounce dried mint

2 tablespoons crushed fennel seeds

1 tablespoon dried lavender flowers

1 cup boiling water

Combine herbs in a sterilized glass jar with a lid. To make tea, add 1 tablespoon of the herbal mixture to a cup (or use a tea ball infuser). Cover the herbs with the boiling water. Let the tea steep for 10 minutes, then strain (if not using a tea ball infuser). Sweeten, if desired. Drink 2 to 4 cups per day.

The more people have studied
different methods of bringing
up children, the more they have
come to the conclusion that
what good mothers and fathers
instinctively feel like doing for their
babies is the best after all.

— Benjamin Spock

CHAPTER 4

TABLE TALK
AND
FINGER
FOOD

CHAPTER 4

As soon as your baby is old enough to sit without support, she's ready to join the family at the dinner table for mealtimes, even if eating solid foods is still a spectator sport for her. But when she becomes interested in learning the skill of fine dining, you'll need to muster up all the patience, encouragement, and clean washcloths you can spare. Here are a few ways to make the transition to solids a pleasant one.

Now, as always, the most
automated appliance in a
household is the mother.

— Beverly Jones

SAFETY COMES FIRST

. . . .

- Make sure your high chair is certified by the Juvenile Products Manufacturers Association (JPMA). This should be identified by a seal on the packaging or on the chair itself. If there is any doubt, contact the JPMA (see Resources) or visit their Web site *www.jpma.org*.

- Always make full use of the restraining belts and straps when your baby is in the high chair. Chairs with removable trays make cleanup easier and will allow you to simply pull the chair up to the table sans the tray when baby is older.

- Never leave your baby unattended in a high chair.

- Don't use bibs that tie around the neck; they present a possible choking hazard. Instead, use bibs with snaps or Velcro tabs that you can easily pull free.

TERRIFIC TIP

If you're caught without a bib and your baby's shirt or top becomes very soiled during a feeding, pull his arms out of the garment and then carefully roll it up before removing it. This will prevent food from adhering to his face or hair.

Older siblings often enjoy helping to spoon-feed their younger brother or sister. But, while this may free your hands for a few moments, don't wander off to another part of the house to do something else. You'll need to supervise the feeding to make sure your older child isn't putting too much food in the baby's mouth at once.

HAVE PATIENCE...AND DON'T FORGET TO DUCK!

....

Expect what you put in to come back out. Babies are messy eaters, but not intentionally. They're used to a liquid diet and at first simply lack the coordination to chew and swallow solid food. Try not to fuss when your baby spits out her food, even if most of her meal lands on the table or floor. However, avoid looking amused when her mashed peas cascade down her chin, or it will become a game. In short, offer simple praises for positive eating habits and try to ignore the negative.

BABY FOOD BASICS

....

Baby's first solid food won't be truly solid — it's more like liquefied versions of adult foodstuffs. Cooked and mashed sweet potatoes, squash, apples, carrots, avocados, bananas, and cereals with liquid added are the standard fare for beginners who are between four and six months of age. Check with your pediatrician for a list of foods and a schedule that's right for your little one.

TERRIFIC TIP

Introduce one new food at a time
and watch for signs of allergy, such
as diarrhea, rashes, or respiratory
problems. The general rule is to let
five days elapse between introducing
different food items.

Whenever possible, select certified organic fruits and vegetables that are free of synthetic pesticides and fertilizers. There are several brands of organic baby food on the market as well. Most supermarkets carry organic foods but, if yours doesn't, you might consider joining a food co-op or growing your own.

Cow's milk is often quite indigestible for humans and is a common source of allergies, especially in the first year. For a healthy alternative, use soy or rice milk (or breast milk) when making cereals or mashed foods.

Make baby food in quantity to be canned or frozen for later use. Homemade baby food will stay fresh in the refrigerator for one to two days and in the freezer for two months. You might want to invest in a canning pot, but any large pot will do to sterilize jars and lids.

Introduce baby to her first table meals after she's had a mini meal from the breast or bottle. This will encourage her to experiment with new foods, and with a little food in her tummy, she'll be less likely to become anxious or frustrated than if she were very hungry.

Babies go through a series of steps in learning to pick up finger foods. At first they use the side of the palm to scoop food pieces toward them. At about six months, babies will begin to draw food pieces to the palm with the fingers but not the thumb. Finally, between six and ten months, babies develop the pincer grasp, in which the thumb and forefinger come together, making the transport of food from hand to mouth more precise.

LEFTY OR RIGHTY?

....

Though infants generally give equal time to both hands, some may ball one hand into a fist more often than the other. However, this isn't really an indication of future handedness. In fact, researchers believe the head may have more to do with it since approximately 70 percent of infants turn their heads to the right more often than to the left and become right-handed. So, if your bundle of joy prefers a left-side view of the world, it may mean that she will be left-handed.

There's no reason to try to sway handedness, just as there's no need to be concerned if you don't observe any preference at all. Which hand will eventually wield the mighty pen won't become fully apparent until the age of four. And a lucky few will have equal dexterity in both hands.

Let baby get a grip. Baby's first spoon for self-feeding should be made from PVC-free plastic, since metal can irritate gums and new teeth. A curved handle allows little hands to get a firm grasp and reduces the risk of a poke to the eye, nose, or nearby sibling.

BABY, FEED THYSELF

....

Just as the transition to solid foods was a milestone for baby, the moment that she begins to feed herself without much help from you is an important step in development. Baby will be tempted to put just about anything in her mouth at this stage, so it's important that you monitor closely what's going in there.

Always watch your baby while she's eating. Food items or pieces should be small enough that they won't become lodged in the throat if swallowed. Before the age of three, don't give baby items such as nuts, raisins, pieces of hard fruit, raw vegetable sticks, and nut butters, which pose a choking hazard.

NATURAL BABY FOOD MADE EASY

....

Why should you prepare homemade baby food? Aside from being less expensive and far superior in taste and nutrition compared to supermarket brands, homemade baby food is blessedly lacking in artificial flavors, colors, and preservatives. A recent study published in the British medical journal *The Lancet* reports that a number of artificial food additives may promote hyperactivity and distractibility in infants and children. In particular, the study referred to one food additive that is commonly found in processed foods: sodium benzoate.

GOOD START CEREAL

....

Simple, nutritious, **and purely delicious!**

> 1 cup rolled oats
>
> ½ cup soy or rice milk (vanilla flavor is good)
>
> ½ cup pure apple juice
>
> ½ banana, mashed

1. Combine all ingredients in a microwave-safe bowl and microwave on high for 2 minutes.

2. For beginning eaters, pour cooked cereal into a blender or food processor and blend with additional soy milk as needed to make a smooth purée.

QUINOA AND SWEET POTATO PORRIDGE

....

Long considered one of the world's most perfect and versatile foods, quinoa is a gluten-free product with a nutty flavor and a texture similar to millet. The addition of sweet potato to this recipe gives the cereal color and sweetness.

> 2 cups water
>
> 1 cup quinoa, rinsed
>
> 1 sweet potato, peeled and cubed

1. Bring the water to a boil. Add the quinoa and sweet potato. Reduce heat and simmer, stirring occasionally, until sweet potato cubes are tender, about 20 minutes.

2. Pour cooked porridge into a blender or food processor and purée. Add a little soy or rice milk to make it smoother.

SPINACH AND CHEESE "SOUFFLÉ"

....

If your child is lactose-intolerant, substitute a combination of ¼ cup of diced tofu and ¼ cup of soy or rice milk mixed in a blender or an egg substitute for the cheeses.

> 1 pound organic spinach, washed
>
> 1 egg, lightly beaten
>
> ½ cup grated parmesan cheese
>
> ¼ cup cottage cheese

1. Place the spinach, still damp, in a nonstick skillet; heat over very low heat until just wilted, about 1 minute.

2. In a large bowl, combine egg, parmesan cheese, and cottage cheese; mix well. Add spinach to the egg-cheese mixture; mix well.

3. Pour the mixture into a lightly greased casserole and bake at 350°F until set, 20 to 30 minutes. Let cool; then purée in a food processor or baby-food grinder to the right consistency for your baby's age.

GUACAMOLE FOR LITTLE PEOPLE

· ·

Avocados are one of nature's perfect ready-made baby foods — they're already packaged for freshness and require no cooking.

> 1 ripe avocado
>
> 1 tablespoon plain yogurt

Peel and mash the avocado with the back of a fork in a small bowl. Add the yogurt and blend well.

OATMEAL WITH SPICED APPLE AND PUMPKIN

....

This smells like a crisp autumn day. Make a double batch so you can share it with baby.

   1 cup cooked oatmeal

   3 tablespoons applesauce

   3 tablespoons pumpkin purée

   dash of cinnamon

Combine all ingredients and stir until blended.

Note: If a finer texture is needed, give the blended cereal a whirl in a blender or food processor for a few seconds.

EGGPLANT SUPREME

....

1 cup steamed or boiled eggplant

Half a banana

Dollop of plain yogurt or soy milk

Purée the eggplant and banana together in a blender or food processor until smooth. Add just enough yogurt or soy milk to the mixture until the desired consistency is reached.

FRESH FRUIT CUSTARD

....

1 cup applesauce

1 cup soy or rice milk

1 mashed banana

4 eggs, beaten (or the equivalent amount
of egg substitute)

1 teaspoon vanilla

1 teaspoon cinnamon

1. Combine all ingredients and mix well in a blender or food processor.

2. Pour mixture into custard cups or ramekins and sprinkle with additional cinnamon if you wish. Set cups into a shallow pan and add hot water to cover 1 inch of the cup bottoms.

3. Bake at 350°F for 45 to 55 minutes, or until a toothpick inserted into the center comes out clean.

4. Chill for at least 1 hour and serve.

Note: The custard will keep in the refrigerator for up to 3 days.

HOMEMADE FRUIT GEL

....

This recipe uses agar obtained from seaweed to help the fruit mixture to thicken and gel. You can find agar flakes in health food stores.

½ cup cool water

1 tablespoon agar flakes

1½ cups fruit juice

1 cup puréed fruit of choice

1. In a small saucepan combine the water with the agar flakes. Stir until the flakes dissolve. Add juice and heat on medium-low heat for about 1 minute, stirring constantly.

2. Pour the mixture into 4 individual ramekins. Place in refrigerator to cool for about 30 minutes. Remove from refrigerator and divide the puréed fruit between the ramekin dishes. Stir well and serve.

FUN WITH FINGER FOODS

....

What can you let your baby feed herself, and when?
Baby-friendly finger foods may be introduced between
7 and 10 months of age, as long as the pincer grasp is
developed. Here are some good first choices:

- Small pieces of soft, seeded fruits (banana, mango,
  peach, watermelon, pear, cantaloupe)

- Cooked, cubed vegetables (carrot, squash, sweet
  potato)

- Chopped hard-boiled eggs

- Toasted whole grain bread cut into small pieces

- Small cooked pasta shapes

Always give your baby just a few bits of food at a time,
or she may put too much in her mouth at once.

BROCCOLI AND CHEESE BITES

The entire family will love these savory snacks!

3 eggs (or substitute equivalent)

2 cups steamed broccoli, chopped

1½ cups shredded cheddar cheese

1 cup bread crumbs

1 teaspoon nutmeg

1 teaspoon oregano

Place all ingredients into a large bowl. Using your hands, combine the ingredients until well blended. Form the mixture into bite-sized rounds and place on a lightly greased baking sheet. Bake at 375°F for 20 to 25 minutes, turning once halfway through baking. Allow to cool before serving.

Note: This recipe calls for whole eggs as a binding agent. If eggs cannot be tolerated due to an allergy, you can use puréed carrots instead, adding a bit of water or vegetable stock to moisten, if needed.

TOFU FINGERS

....

These little treats pack a punch of protein and savory flavor. Watch them disappear!

    1 package firm tofu, drained

    1 tablespoon tamari

    1 cup wheat germ

    1 tablespoon sesame seeds

    1 cup plain bread crumbs

1. Slice tofu into small strips; using a basting brush, lightly coat tofu pieces with tamari.

2. In a blender or food processor, grind the wheat germ and sesame seeds for one minute. On a plate, combine the ground wheat germ and sesame seed mixture with the bread crumbs.

3. Roll the tofu fingers in the crumb mixture and place on a lightly oiled baking sheet. Bake at 350°F for 15 to 20 minutes, until golden brown.

TAKE CARE OF THOSE NEW TEETH

....

Some babies sprout a tooth or two without any problem at all — much to the surprise of their parents when making the discovery one morning! Other babies seem to get one tooth at a time for an agonizing eternity. But the teething process is usually steady and spans anywhere from three months to three years of age.

Some signs that your baby is teething include the appearance of red cheeks, a temporary loss of appetite, irritability (you won't miss this one), and increased drooling (although three-month-olds typically drool a fair amount anyway). Contrary to popular belief, teething is never indicated by fever. If fever is present, take it as a sign of illness.

PROTECT THOSE PEARLY WHITES

....

Avoid dental problems before they start. Never let your baby go to sleep with a bottle, even if it's water. Bacteria can linger on the nipple, and liquid may find its way to the inner ear causing ear infections.

Keep new teeth clean. The time to begin a cleaning regimen begins as soon as the first tooth has emerged. You can clean a sole tooth or a scant few with a damp washcloth or piece of gauze wrapped around your finger. When several teeth appear, it's time for a baby toothbrush.

Do not use commercial toothpaste until your child is at least two (in part due to the fluoride content and because your child will likely swallow it), but after that, you can use natural unsweetened toothpaste that does not contain fluoride. Check with your dentist or pediatrician.

Give baby foods to teethe by. A frozen popsicle (all natural and without sweeteners, please) or a frozen banana can work wonders on sore gums. But be sure to remove the item when it begins to thaw; otherwise, small pieces could begin to break off, presenting a choking hazard.

Older babies and toddlers might prefer hard toast or biscuits, but again, make sure there's no danger of choking. If the biscuit contains sugar, clean baby's teeth soon after eating, or at least have her drink some water until you can clean them. Always make sure your baby is sitting upright when teething on foods, and remain nearby to supervise.

Teething rings can seem like a lifesaving toy for both you and your baby. Get the kind that you can fill with water and freeze. The coolness will ease painful inflammation of the gums while the hardness will help the tooth make its escape to the surface.

Note: Make sure the teething ring is PVC free.

O young thing, your mother's lovely armful! How sweet the fragrance of your body!

— Euripides

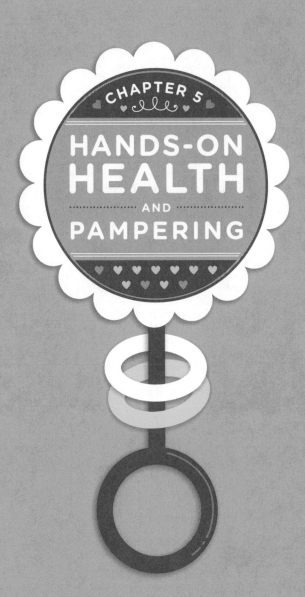

CHAPTER 5

HANDS-ON HEALTH

AND

PAMPERING

CHAPTER 5

Babies need special care and pampering to ensure optimum health. Sensitive newborn skin and hair, for instance, deserve to be cared for with pure and natural ingredients to stay healthy without risking exposure to chemicals and preservatives. You can also keep your baby happy and healthy with simple, natural remedies for everyday common ailments.

While you're pampering baby at home, your pediatrician will be busy monitoring your child's progress in terms of weight gain and physical development. During the first year of life, your baby is learning to control the movements of his arms and legs. At first, these movements may seem to occur without meaningful deliberation or purpose. However, practicing movement is how your baby learns to synchronize his brain, eyes, and hands. You can help those little gray cells and muscles along with a few simple (and fun!) strengthening exercises.

Though motherhood is the most important of all the professions — requiring more knowledge than any other department in human affairs — there was no attention given to preparation for this office.

— Elizabeth Cady Stanton

Turn baby loose on her tummy. Young babies need daily time on their tummies to develop upper body strength and motor skills. This is particularly necessary to coordinate control over the muscles involving the neck and head.

A cloth exercise mat is ideal for this purpose. In addition to the convenience of being machine washable, cloth exercise mats are usually made from fabric panels of varying color and texture to provide tactile stimulation during tummy time exercise.

Try baby's version of the "medicine ball." Place baby on her stomach on a beach ball and carefully rock her back and forth while supporting her with one hand. Not only is this fun for baby, but it might help to dislodge a gas bubble or two.

BABY GYMNASTICS

....

While baby lies on his back, gently hold his arms at his sides. Alternate raising one arm over his head and then the other. While you're at it, you can teach the Newtonian principle of what goes up must come down by chanting "Up we go, down we go" with each movement.

Encourage baby to reach out. When she is able to grasp and let go of an object, hold an enticing toy just within her reach. It helps to focus her attention if the toy is a noisemaker or is brightly colored.

Do the baby bicycle. Gently grasp your baby's feet and move them in bicycle fashion as though he is pedaling. It won't take long before baby is able to do this exercise on his own.

By the time baby is three months old, she'll be able to prop herself up on her forearms, as well as lift her head and chest off the floor. You can help her to develop upper body strength by encouraging her to reach for an object so that she has to shift weight from one forearm to the other.

By six months of age, baby is ready to become adept at rolling from one side to the other while lying on her back. She'll also begin to start reaching for her toes while practicing this movement. Help her to enjoy this activity even more by gently tickling the soles of her feet. Soon she'll master reaching for her feet while rolling so well that she'll one day discover how to sit up unassisted.

When your baby is at least three months old and can support his own head, he can do "sit-ups." While holding baby's hands, gently pull him to a sitting position and then lower him back to the floor.

You can create a baby "Stairmaster" by allowing your 9- to 12-month-old to crawl up your staircase (with close supervision) or over a stack of pillows.

WHY GO ALL NATURAL?

In a word: phthalates. A recent study published in the journal *Pediatrics* revealed that commercial cosmetics formulated for infants contain high levels of phthalates, toxic agents that are used in the plastics industry. Specifically, phthalates are used to make hard plastic more flexible. The study found that infant lotions were the biggest culprit, resulting in the highest concentration of phthalates being detected in infant urine. However, other products designed for topical use, such as baby shampoo and baby powder, were also found to contain unsafe levels of phthalates. These toxic agents have been linked to reproductive disorders in humans.

Here are some other ingredients found in many commercial skin care products:

- Lauramide DEA—Used as a thickening agent, it's associated with skin disorders and allergic reactions.

- Sodium laurel sulfate and sodium laureth sulfate—Found in many lotions, these chemicals are highly irritating.

- Propylene glycol—This is a common skin allergen.

- Mineral oil and petroleum products—These substances clog pores and deprive cells of oxygen.

PAMPERING BABY'S SKIN

....

Babies have such soft, sweet-smelling skin — they deserve equally tender, mild skin care. With a few simple ingredients from your local herb or health food store you can make your own all-natural skin formulas to use after your baby's bath (page 155), while diapering (page 175), and even to protect against sunburn (page 185). The whole family will want to use them! They make great gifts for other babies and parents, too.

TERRIFIC TIP

Homemade formulas are very mild, but it's always wise to perform a patch test before using a new product on your baby's skin. Apply a small amount of the product to baby's inner arm, just above the elbow. Wait 24 hours; if any itching, redness, or other signs of irritation occur, discontinue use immediately.

BEAUTIFUL BABY BALM

....

Use this balm during diaper changes to protect baby's skin.

½ ounce cocoa butter

½ ounce beeswax

1 tablespoon jojoba oil

1 tablespoon glycerin

1 tablespoon rosewater (available in pharmacies)

4 drops chamomile essential oil

4 drops mandarin essential oil

1. In a double boiler set over medium heat, combine cocoa butter, beeswax, and jojoba oil; heat until completely melted. Add glycerin and rosewater; stir.

2. Remove from heat and add essential oils. Scoop into a sterilized jar and label. Store at room temperature and away from heat and drafts. Discard any unused portion after 6 weeks.

NATURAL BABY OIL

Use this oil on baby's damp skin after a bath.

> 6 drops calendula essential oil
>
> 2 drops lavender essential oil
>
> 2 drops rose essential oil
>
> 1 bottle (4 ounces) sweet almond oil

Add the essential oils directly to the bottle of sweet almond oil. Shake well before using. This formula will keep its effectiveness for up to a year. A bottle this size should last for about six months with normal use.

SKIN SO SILKY

....

This formula is very nourishing for skin and suitable for use by every member of the family.

> 1 cup sweet almond oil
>
> ½ cup cocoa butter
>
> 2 teaspoons lanolin
>
> ½ ounce beeswax
>
> ⅔ cup rosewater
>
> ½ cup aloe vera gel
>
> 6 drops rose essential oil
>
> contents of 2 vitamin E capsules

1. In a double boiler set over medium heat, combine the sweet almond oil, cocoa butter, lanolin, and beeswax; heat until completely melted. Remove from heat and add remaining ingredients.

2. Mix with an electric mixer until smooth and creamy. Scoop into a sterilized jar and label. Store away from heat. Discard any unused portion after 6 weeks.

MAKING SCENTS FOR BABY

Smell is the only sense that is fully developed in humans at birth. It's not surprising that babies respond quite readily to aromatherapy. A diffuser comes in handy when using essential oils for aromatherapy, but keep in mind that essential oils should never be used "neat" (undiluted) in a diffuser in a baby's room. Their concentration is too strong for little lungs. Instead, dilute the essential oil in a base oil, such as jojoba or sweet almond.

SCENTS-ABILITIES

....

Here's the simplest way to use aromatherapy in a small baby's nursery: Add the essential oils to water in a simmer pot or even to a small pan of warm water (about 1 cup); place the pot or pan in the room out of the reach of baby, siblings, and pets.

Note: If you're using a diffuser, dilute the essential oils in 2 tablespoons of base oil.

The following combinations are especially soothing:

- *Nursing Aide:* 1 drop each of chamomile, dill, and sweet orange essential oils.

- *Stuffy Nose Relief:* 1 drop of lemon essential oil and 2 drops of eucalyptus essential oil.

- *Sleepy Time Formula:* 1 drop each of chamomile and dill essential oils.

TERRIFIC TIP

Always use pure botanical essential oils instead of synthetic fragrance oils; the latter often contain alcohols and other irritants. Avoid oils sold in clear glass or plastic as these containers expose the product to light and cause it to degrade.

GUIDE TO USING ESSENTIAL OILS FOR AROMATHERAPY

AGE	AMOUNT
Under 2 months	1–3 drops, diluted
2–12 months	3–5 drops, diluted
1–2 years	5–10 drops, diluted

The essential oils listed below are gentle and safe for use around babies and young children. Please remember that essential oils are highly concentrated and should always be diluted, whether in a diffuser or on the skin. Also, essential oils should never be used internally.

- *Calendula*: a natural deodorizer
- *Chamomile*: soothing, improves a variety of skin conditions
- *Dill*: has a calming effect and is traditionally used to induce sleep in babies
- *Lavender*: relaxing, has antiviral and anti-inflammatory properties
- *Mandarin*: invigorating, reduces tension
- *Neroli*: enhances mood, has mild sedative effects
- *Rose*: relaxing, enhances mood
- *Sweet orange*: a natural, soothing antiseptic
- *Yarrow*: has astringent qualities, reduces inflammation

A DELICATE AREA

....

When you think about it, the umbilical cord is an amazing thing. But once the cord is cut and tied after birth, it looks a lot less interesting as it shrivels on your baby's belly on its way to becoming a navel. For the most part, Mother Nature takes care of this process herself so don't do anything to treat it for at least 24 hours. But since infection is a possibility, you'll want to keep the area dry and free of bacteria until the final remains of the cord wither and drop off, usually within 7 to 10 days.

HELP IN HEALING

....

Make your own herbal antiseptic powder. Combine a cup of cornstarch (or arrowroot powder) and 2 teaspoons of pure, ground thyme. After bathing, dust the area around the cord with a cotton ball dipped in this powder.

Note: Always shield baby's face to prevent inhalation of powders.

Lavender has antibacterial properties and speeds the healing of skin. Mix 1 tablespoon of distilled water with 1 drop of lavender essential oil. Dip a cotton ball into the mixture and gently clean the area around the umbilical cord.

Soothe flaky, dry skin around the cord with this formula: 2 tablespoons of sweet almond oil, 3 drops of chamomile essential oil, and 1 drop of rose essential oil. Massage 2–3 drops into the skin twice a day. Incidentally, this formula may also help improve irregular skin pigmentation on other parts of the body, although birthmarks will only fade with time, if at all.

GIVE CRADLE CAP THE BRUSH-OFF

....

Cradle cap is not a disease, but is actually a sign of healthy skin growth. In adults, new skin cells are generated at about the same rate as old ones die and are shed. But in infants, new skin cells often grow at a faster rate than the old, creating these telltale greasy, scaly patches.

Cradle cap is very common, but it's rather unsightly when it comes off in large clumps or layers. And although your baby can't tell you directly if it feels uncomfortable, it seems likely that it could be itchy. Here are some simple ways to alleviate this bothersome condition.

To help soften cradle cap, massage in a few drops of this infused oil before shampooing: Blend 2 tablespoons of sweet almond oil with 1 drop each of calendula and geranium essential oils. For best results, use this formula once each day, taking care around the fontanelle, or "soft spot," until all of the secretions disappear.

A natural after-shampoo rinse made from a cooled infusion of comfrey is also helpful. Bring 1 quart of water and 1 ounce of sliced dried comfrey root to a boil. Simmer for 20 to 30 minutes; then strain, reserving the liquid. Apply to the area using a washcloth, gently loosening crusty patches. This rinse will keep in the refrigerator for up to a week, but let it sit out for a few hours to return to room temperature before using.

TERRIFIC TIP

A soft, natural-bristle brush is not only good for a young baby's hair (if she has any!), but also helpful for loosening and removing cradle cap. Using a 100% cotton washcloth on your baby's scalp while bathing will also help to loosen and remove crusty spots.

COCOA BUTTER AND SLIPPERY ELM FORMULA

....

This formula is simple to make and has a relatively long shelf life. Slippery elm bark is high in mucilage, which will help to loosen cradle cap's grip on the scalp.

¼ cup sweet almond oil

2 tablespoons powdered slippery elm bark

1 tablespoon pure cocoa butter

1. In a nonstick saucepan over low heat, gently heat the sweet almond oil and slippery elm bark for 5 to 10 minutes, until warm and mixed well. Add cocoa butter; stirring constantly, heat 5 minutes longer.

2. Strain the mixture through a mesh strainer into a sterilized widemouthed jar; let stand until cool. Refrigerate until the mixture is completely solid; then store in a cool, dry place.

3. Apply the solid paste with your fingertips to areas with cradle cap before shampooing, gently rubbing with a washcloth or soft brush to loosen crusty patches. Discard any unused portion after 6 weeks.

THE HERBAL BATH

....

Herbal baths are relaxing and therapeutic. To a full tub of warm water, add a drop (and only one drop) of one of the following essential oils:

- *Chamomile*
- *Geranium*
- *Lavender*
- *Yarrow*

Distribute the oil in the water with your fingers before putting your baby in the tub.

Alternately, you can add the essential oil to a cup of milk (a great softening agent!) before adding it to the bath water. You can also use a cup of cooled herbal tea in place of the essential oil.

Condition your baby's skin with an infused herbal oil. Blend 1 teaspoon of sweet almond oil or hazelnut oil with a drop of chamomile, lavender, or yarrow essential oil and add to baby's bath water, dispersing the mixture into the water well with your fingers.

THE LURE OF LAVENDER

....

The aroma of lavender does more than lull baby to sleep. According to a study published in the journal *Early Human Development*, babies bathed in lavender-infused water looked at their mothers more often, slept more deeply, and cried less. The mothers involved in the study benefited, too, as evidenced by a decrease in levels of the stress-related hormone cortisol, which resulted in greater relaxation and an increased touching of their infants.

HERBAL BATH BAG

....

Bath bags are one of the easiest and most inexpensive herbal preparations you can make. Herbal baths are so soothing you'll want to use this recipe for yourself! (For a regular-sized tub, make a bigger bag or use two of the baby-sized ones described here.)

> 1 medium square of cotton cloth (about the size of a washcloth)
>
> 2 tablespoons fresh or dried lavender, chamomile, lemon balm, calendula, yarrow, or dill (or a combination of several)
>
> One 6- to 8-inch length of ribbon or string

1. Place the herbs in the center of the cloth; bring the corners up to the center to form a bag. Firmly secure the top with the ribbon or string.

2. Place the bath bag in a tub of warm water. Let the herbs infuse in the bath water for at least 5 minutes. Remove the bag before placing baby in the tub.

DIAPER RASH RESCUE

....

Diaper rash feels as painful to your baby as it looks to you. Frequent diaper changes are necessary to prevent a rash from getting a foothold. But avoid using petroleum-based creams; though they might form an effective barrier from moisture, they aren't good for your baby's skin. Instead, try these natural methods for preventing and treating diaper rash.

TERRIFIC TIP

For older babies, sunshine is one of the best cures for diaper rash. When the weather permits, let your little one expose her bum to the early-morning or late-afternoon sun. Apply sunscreen first and limit the exposure time to about 10 minutes to prevent sunburn!

SKIN SAVERS

....

Here is a great alternative to commercial baby wipes:

1. Fill a sterilized widemouthed canning jar with a solution of 1 cup of water, 2 drops of lavender essential oil, and 1 drop of chamomile essential oil.

2. Add multiple folded squares of pure cotton or cellulose sponge to the jar.

3. Shake well and store at room temperature.

4. To use, remove a cloth, squeeze out any excess liquid, and gently wipe over baby's skin. Wash and reuse these wipes whenever possible.

DIAPER RASH PREVENTION CREAM

....

½ cup 100 percent pure aloe vera gel

½ cup cocoa butter

2 tablespoons jojoba or sweet almond oil

contents of 3 vitamin E capsules

6 drops calendula essential oil

1. In a small saucepan, combine the aloe vera gel, cocoa butter, and jojoba or sweet almond oil. Heat on very low heat, stirring constantly, until the cocoa butter is completely melted. Stir in the contents of the vitamin E capsules and mix well.

2. Remove from heat and let cool for 5 minutes; then stir again. Blend in the calendula essential oil.

3. Pour the mixture into small sterile glass jars and let cool completely before capping. Needs no refrigeration; lasts for 6 to 8 months.

PAMPER WITH POWDER

....

Commercial baby powders can include questionable ingredients, including synthetic fragrances that can cause irritation. Once again, simple ingredients can replace those that nature didn't intend for your baby.

Talcum powder, or talc, is a common ingredient in body powders, but it's not the best to use on your baby. Talc is extremely fine, easily inhaled, and can lead to chemical pneumonia. It can also contain minute traces of arsenic.

Better choices for making simple, absorbent powders for your baby include cornstarch, arrowroot powder, French clay, rice flour, and powdered herbal flowers such as elder, chamomile, lavender, and calendula.

TERRIFIC TIP

When using powders on your baby, always shield his face to prevent accidental inhalation. In fact, it's a good idea to put the powder in your hand before powdering his bottom.

HEALING BABY POWDER

....

The lavender essential oil used in this formula will reduce redness and inflammation caused by skin irritations and prevent the occurrence of diaper rash.

Note: This powder is also an excellent one for parents to use during warm weather on areas such as underarms and feet.

> 2 cups cornstarch
>
> 2 cups arrowroot powder
>
> 3 tablespoons French clay
>
> ½ cup powdered calendula flowers
>
> 6 drops lavender essential oil

In a large mixing bowl, blend the cornstarch, arrowroot powder, French clay, and calendula flowers. Sprinkle the essential oil into the mixture and blend well. Store the finished powder in tins, small glass jars, or plastic containers with shaker tops. Your supply should last about 6 months.

SILKY BABY BLEND

This formula will protect baby's skin from excess moisture and leave it feeling silky smooth. The addition of aloe vera powder (available in health food stores and online) speeds healing of minor skin irritations. The chamomile and lavender essential oils work together to produce a calming effect as well.

> 3 cups cornstarch
>
> 2 cups French clay
>
> ½ cup aloe vera powder
>
> ½ cup powdered lavender flowers
>
> 4 drops chamomile essential oil
>
> 2 drops lavender essential oil

In a large mixing bowl, blend the cornstarch, French clay, aloe vera powder, and lavender flowers. Sprinkle the essential oils into the mixture and blend well. Store the powder in tins, small glass jars, or plastic containers with shaker tops. Your supply should last about 6 months.

CHASE AWAY COLIC

Trapped gas is painful for your baby, and its occurrence can challenge you long into the night, too. A colicky baby appears to be in pain and may cry for long periods. He might draw his legs up in discomfort. He might be able to release a few gas blasts on his own, but there are some simple things you can do to help things along.

WHAT A RELIEF!

....

A baby might find relief if you place her on her tummy and rub the small of her back in rhythmic, circular motions.

Baby bicycle movements can work wonders to release gas. Gently hold your baby's ankles and slowly move his legs as though pedaling a bike.

If you are nursing, consider whether or not your diet is causing your baby's gas. Beans and certain vegetables, such as broccoli and asparagus, are notorious gas producers. If you're bottle-feeding, make sure the nipple is properly positioned and that the baby is held slightly upright to prevent her from taking in too much air.

Massage baby with the "waterwheel" stroke. With baby lying on his back, gently stroke his stomach with warm, lightly oiled palms. Each hand should glide and pass over the other.

COLIC RELIEF
MASSAGE OIL

....

Dill has long been used to soothe colic and to help babies get to sleep. The aroma of this formula is reminiscent of the old-fashioned "gripe" water sometimes given to colicky babies.

1 drop dill essential oil

1 tablespoon sweet almond oil

Blend the oils together in a small cup. Spread the oil on your hands and rub your hands together briskly to warm them before massaging your baby.

SUN SAFETY

....

Young children need extra protection from the sun's rays. When baby is going to be in the sun, be sure to safeguard her delicate skin with either a sunscreen or a sunblock. What's the difference between these products? Sunblocks contain mineral salts such as titanium dioxide that reflect the sun's rays away from tender skin. Sunscreens allow for the absorption of a small amount of ultraviolet (UV) rays, but filters them into harmless infrared wavelengths.

Also limit exposure. Babies less than one year old can burn quite easily. And if they're very young, they cannot escape the sun by crawling away or express to you that they've been exposed too long. Never leave a baby sitting on a blanket or in a stroller in direct sunlight for more than 10 minutes.

Use natural products, but be aware of what they contain. The only sunscreen component that is natural and approved by the Food and Drug Administration (FDA) is para-aminobenzoic acid (PABA), a vitamin B derivative. Commercial sunscreen products commonly include octyl methoxycinnamate (obtained from cinnamon or cassia), octyl salicylate (derived from sweet birch, wintergreen, and willow), and other botanicals that offer anti-inflammatory or antioxidant qualities, such as aloe vera, black walnut, milk thistle, green tea extract, chamomile, eucalyptus, and mint.

MOMMY'S BEST SUNSCREEN OIL

....

Sesame seed oil is a natural sunscreen and nourishing to skin as well. The whole family will enjoy using this formula.

> ½ cup cocoa butter
>
> ¼ cup aloe vera gel
>
> ¼ cup sesame oil
>
> ¼ cup sweet almond oil
>
> contents of 5 vitamin E capsules
>
> 10 drops lavender essential oil
>
> 8 drops chamomile essential oil

1. In a saucepan or double boiler set over low heat, combine cocoa butter, aloe vera gel, sesame oil, and sweet almond oil. Heat just until the cocoa butter has melted. Remove from heat.

2. Add vitamin E and essential oils; stir well. Let cool completely.

3. Pour the cooled mixture into two or three small recycled plastic squirt bottles. Shake before each use. Store unrefrigerated; discard after 4 months.

TERRIFIC TIP

Make baby fashionable. Give her a snazzy sun hat with a visor to shield her scalp and face. It's even more fun if you wear one that matches!

If a burn should occur, combine 2 teaspoons of sweet almond oil and 1 drop of lavender essential oil and gently rub it into baby's skin. Or apply a small amount of 100 percent pure aloe vera gel to the area.

Here's another soothing burn remedy: Fill baby's bath with equal amounts of warm water and apple cider vinegar. The vinegar helps reduce redness and pain and restores the pH mantle of the skin. Be careful not to let this solution get in baby's eyes!

A CLEAN BABY IS
A HAPPY BABY

....

Nothing could be simpler than creating these all-natural soaps. To make them last longer, let them dry out between uses.

> 3 bars unscented castile soap, grated
>
> 2 tablespoons sweet almond oil
>
> 1½ tablespoons lanolin
>
> 3 tablespoons ground oatmeal
>
> 2 tablespoons dried, crushed lavender
> (leaves and flowers)
>
> 6 drops lavender essential oil

1. In a double boiler set over medium heat, heat the soap, sweet almond oil, and lanolin until completely melted, stirring occasionally. Remove from heat and stir in remaining ingredients.

2. With oiled hands, scoop up small amounts of the soap mixture and form balls about the size of a lemon. Place the soap balls on waxed paper and let stand until completely cooled and hardened.

GLYCERIN HERBAL SOAP

....

Glycerin bars are very gentle and moisturizing, and they can be found in almost any supermarket or pharmacy. These soaps will disappear quickly if left in a puddle of water in the soap dish, so keep them dry between uses.

> 3 bars glycerin soap, unscented
>
> 1 tablespoon sweet almond oil
>
> 5 drops rose essential oil

1. Chop the glycerin soap into chucks with a sharp knife and melt completely in a double boiler set over medium heat. Remove from heat; blend in the oils.

2. Pour the mixture into ungreased soap molds. (These are available in craft stores in fun shapes.) You can also use small, clean plastic containers or lids as molds. If you pop the molds into the freezer, they'll be set in 30 to 45 minutes. When completely cool, tap out the soaps and wrap in tissue paper, wax paper, or clean cloth until ready to use.

PURE AND SIMPLE
BODY WASH AND SHAMPOO

....

It doesn't get any simpler than this! Pure castile soap is made from coconut or olive oil and is very gentle.

> 4 drops chamomile essential oil
>
> 2 drops lavender essential oil
>
> 1 bottle (16 ounces) liquid castile soap, unscented

1. Place the essential oils in the container of castile soap. Replace the lid and shake well.

2. To use as a body wash, just squeeze out a teaspoonful onto a moist cotton washcloth. You can also use this formula as a shampoo, but be careful not to let it get into baby's eyes.

TERRIFIC TIP

Herbal creams and soaps make wonderful shower gifts — mix up an extra batch for an expectant friend.

BASIC BABY FIRST AID

....

Always consult with your health care practitioner when your baby shows signs of illness. An infant's immune, digestive, and respiratory systems are under-developed, and it is inappropriate to treat any related disorder yourself. But for outward bumps, bruises, minor cuts, and rashes, there are a few simple and natural remedies you can use to promote healing.

Note: These treatments should be used only on children older than three months.

EASY AT-HOME REMEDIES

....

Bee stings: Make a cold compress by dipping a cloth in a solution of ½ cup of cold water, ½ cup of cider vinegar, and 2 drops of chamomile essential oil. Apply the compress to the affected area for several minutes. If allergic reactions (such as swelling of extremities) to the bee sting appear, seek medical attention immediately.

Bruises: Arnica (*Arnica montana*), commonly known as mountain daisy, is a member of the aster family. Arnica reduces pain and inflammation; it is available in gel and spray form from your natural health food store. Arnica is toxic, however, so never use it on broken skin and keep it out of reach of children and pets.

Burns: To treat a minor burn, blend 1 teaspoon of sweet almond oil with 1 drop of lavender essential oil and smooth over the area. Or squeeze a bit of juice from an aloe vera plant and rub it on the skin.

Scrapes and cuts: In a double boiler set over low heat, slowly melt 2 tablespoons of beeswax, 1 tablespoon of shea butter, and 1 teaspoon of glycerin (available from pharmacies or craft stores). Remove from heat and stir in the contents of 2 vitamin E capsules and 1 drop each of lavender, chamomile, and yarrow essential oils. Pour the mixture into a sterilized jar and let cool completely before using. Apply lightly to affected areas.

BE GOOD TO YOURSELF

....

If you don't take good care of yourself, it will be harder to take good care of your baby. It's no secret that your body's demands during pregnancy and childbirth can lead to fatigue. During this time, everyday stress can take a toll on your and your baby's health and well-being.

You might be surprised to find that it's not the big stuff that can wear you down, like a change of residence or preparing to leave your job; it's the accumulated total of all the little things that you face every day, like household chores, financial responsibilities, and wondering if you'll ever have a waistline again. When you find yourself sweating the small stuff, try the easy stress reducers on the next few pages.

RELAXATION THERAPY

....

Not only do regular walks help to bring you back into psychological balance, but also the exercise will benefit both you and your baby. If possible, walk in natural environments such as parks or a wooded path.

Clear your mind with relaxation tapes or soothing instrumental music. Take a moment to meditate and relax your body. With your eyes closed, take in long, deep breaths through your mouth; then exhale slowly through your nostrils. As you exhale, concentrate on a single thought or image; try repeating a single word to yourself (such as "one") or imagining that you can "see" through your forehead.

TAKE A LOAD OFF

....

Treat yourself to an herbal foot soak. To a small plastic tub of warm water add 3 to 6 drops of lavender essential oil or a cup of fresh lavender flowers. You can also add several small, round pebbles to the tub and massage your feet over them while you soak.

Need a quick fix for stress? Just place one drop of lavender or rose essential oil on a tissue or cotton cloth and inhale when needed. A scented hankie travels well, too. See page 161 for more information on using essential oils.

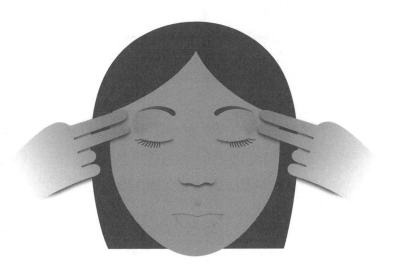

Give yourself a soothing facial massage. Combine a teaspoon of sweet almond oil or jojoba oil with a drop of chamomile or lavender essential oil and blend well. Using your fingertips, massage the mixture around your temples, jaw line, cheekbones, and brow line.

Note: Most experts recommend that essential oils should not be used during the first three months of pregnancy.

AROMATHERAPY FOR BALANCE

These formulas are intended to be inhaled, not applied to the skin.

For emotional/mental stress: 1 drop each of bergamot, sandalwood, and geranium essential oils

For fatigue: 1 drop each of rosemary, chamomile, and lavender essential oils

To beat the "blues": 1 drop each of nutmeg, lemon, and frankincense essential oils

For muscle aches: 1 drop each of chamomile, geranium, and jasmine essential oils

For nausea: 1 drop each of fennel, coriander, and cardamom essential oils

To calm: 1 drop each of cedar, sweet orange, and chamomile essential oils

To stimulate: 1 drop each of eucalyptus, lemon, and rosemary essential oils

GOOD FOR WHAT AILS YOU

....

Pregnancy is wonderful, but it can be tough on your body. Try these simple remedies for some familiar problems.

Stretch Mark Reducer: Blend 2 ounces of sweet almond oil, 1 ounce of wheat germ oil, 8 drops of borage seed oil, 6 drops of carrot essential oil, and 3 drops of rose essential oil. Lightly massage onto the breasts, buttocks, and thighs once daily.

Varicose Vein Therapy: Blend together 1 ounce of carrier oil (such as avocado or sweet almond), 4 drops of geranium essential oil, and 2 drops of cypress essential oil. Lightly massage the oil into the legs, working from the ankle to the thigh. *Note:* Some women should not massage varicose veins; check with your doctor first.

Hemorrhoid Help: Blend 4 drops of carrier oil (such as avocado or sweet almond) with 1 drop of cypress essential oil and 2 drops of myrrh essential oil. Spread the mixture around the anal area to relieve discomfort as needed.

Children as living arrows
are sent forth.

— Kahlil Gibran

BABIES
ARE BORN
LEARNERS

Babies are like sponges; they are willing to absorb everything. In fact, half of an infant's brain growth occurs in the first six months of life, up to 85 percent in the first year. The first year of learning affects not only their mental development but their personality traits as well.

It's not advisable to try to mold your baby into a neurosurgeon or Nobel Prize winner with slide shows and documentaries, but there are simple things you can do each day to improve his quality of mental stimulation. Spending time with your baby in this way will also help to develop a strong bond between the two of you that will last long after his childhood toys and trinkets are put away.

Mother, let us imagine we are
traveling, and passing through a
strange and dangerous country.

— Rabindranath Tagore

TURN OFF THE TUBE

....

In many households, background "white noise" generated from a television is commonplace. However, researchers have recently verified something mothers have suspected for some time — television, even if it's not being watched, inhibits learning. The American Academy of Pediatrics recommends that children under the age of three, infants in particular, spend zero hours in front of the tube.

For many parents, this seems unrealistic, if not downright impossible. Still, it is wise to limit the amount of television your older baby or toddler watches. When a program does warrant viewing, try to watch it with your child and talk about what's happening on screen. Doing so affords an opportunity for enhanced learning and an exchange of ideas (even with a preverbal child) and more cuddle time.

Speak baby's language. Studies have shown that infants pay more attention to baby talk than regular speech. Child development professionals call this "child-directed speech," but we know it as cooing. Imitating your baby's goo-goos and ga-gas shows baby that you take an interest in her. Engaging in two-way baby talk is also important for emotional bonding and cognitive development.

INTRODUCE NATURAL WONDERS

....

The natural world is like a fine tapestry crafted from living thread, a place of continual wonderment. Teaching your baby simple ways to appreciate nature will encourage responsible citizenship on this big blue marble of ours. You might even learn, or relearn, a few things yourself!

Romance your baby in the moonlight. On a clear night, step outside to observe the glow of the moon and the twinkling of the stars. Teach him "Twinkle, twinkle, little star" and make a wish together.

Stop and smell the roses. Babies delight in smelling different things. Grow an aromatic flower garden and let baby sample all the different scents it has to offer. Or tour public gardens and parks with beautiful plantings.

At home, encourage her to smell the different ingredients as you make dinner. Spices and herbs offer a wonder variety of scents — just make sure she doesn't inhale any powdered versions (especially pepper!).

On a breezy day, lie on your backs on a blanket and watch the clouds roll by and change shapes.

If a child is to keep his inborn sense of wonder, he needs the companionship of at least one adult who can share it, rediscovering with him the joy, excitement, and mystery of the world we live in.

— Rachel Carson

Entire biosystems live right under our feet. Since baby spends much of her time close to the ground, there are plenty of living wonders to observe. Point out how an ant can carry a crumb three times its size back to its nest. Show her how to lightly brush a finger along the length of a fuzzy caterpillar or to feel the moss growing up the side of a tree. One day, she'll be making new discoveries about the natural world all on her own.

Nurture baby's growing brain with play. Select toys and activities that will promote active learning, exploration, age-appropriate problem solving, and a sense of accomplishment. Toys such as discovery books or play mats entertain baby while she learns about the world by "discovering" their hidden secrets. These experiences may include finding a ladybug resting under a leaf-shaped flap of felt, looking at bold images of animals against a high-contrast pattern, or feeling different textures.

Take your time discovering these objects with your baby. You can help her to identify specific objects by name or even make up stories about them.

NAPS INCREASE ABSTRACT LEARNING

....

You might appreciate a rest during the afternoon, but your baby actually *needs* regular daytime naps to engage in abstract learning, or the ability to recognize patterns in sights and sounds that are necessary for cognitive development. Researchers at the University of Arizona tested this theory by subjecting infants to a series of sounds intended to mimic predictive phrases used in language.

While these phrases sounded like gibberish, they were constructed of three distinct components that presented a relationship between the first and last phrase. The babies that napped paid more attention than those that didn't nap. In fact, the rested babies were able to remember and recognize previously heard sounds and apply the learned relationship between them to recognizing predictive patterns when new phrases were introduced.

BE BABY'S FIRST TEACHER

....

Babies 12 months and older are beginning to view the world beyond their own existence. Encourage a broad worldview with books, music, videos, and events that embrace cultural and racial diversity. Teaching tolerance and acceptance now will have a lasting impact.

Engage your baby in activities that involve all the senses as much as possible.

- Smell things.

- Encourage laughter and song.

- Compare the textures of different everyday objects.

- Let her crawl or walk barefoot in grass and sand.

- Give her a spoon and a bunch of different objects to tap on.

Babies aged 6 to 12 months adore imitating sounds and facial expressions. Make a game of making the appropriate sound when looking at animal pictures. Let him see your facial expressions often; this is one of the earliest forms of communication he'll use.

Seize opportunities for learning, or create them yourself.

- Point out different colors and shapes or recite the ABC's while you and your baby are sitting in traffic or waiting for a doctor's appointment.

- Talk about the things you see while walking around the neighborhood.

- Tell him what you're doing as you prepare a meal or give him a bath.

BABY'S COLORS

....

What's black, white, and red all over? A newborn can see your face from a distance of about six inches, but until six to eight weeks of age, she cannot distinguish its features. And while adults may find the traditional pastel colors of "pretty in pink" and "baby-boy blue" appealing, your baby cannot see in full color until she's about four months old.

Black, white, and red pictures and objects displayed against a high-contrast background on rattles, play mats, blankets, mobiles, and activity centers are designed to challenge infants under the age of four months.

Don't go overboard with the stimulation. Your baby will let you know when she's had enough by crying or simply looking away from you. Take these gestures as a signal that it's time to cuddle instead.

GAMES BABIES PLAY

....

Playtime is learning time for your baby, and until he's two or three, you are his primary and favorite playmate. Here are some silly games to make you both giggle.

Babies up to six months love the "I'm gonna getcha" game. From a short distance, slowly "stalk" baby while chanting "I'm gonna getcha!" At first, baby may look puzzled, even alarmed, but he'll soon get the pattern and realize that he can trust you. It's even better if the final "getcha" is accompanied with a raspberry to the neck or a gentle tickle to the tummy.

Try the bumblebee surprise. Raise your hand with one finger extended and slowly make your way down to baby's belly, spiraling as you go and making a "z-z-z" sound. When you've reached your target, move in for the "sting" by gently poking his belly.

The traditional peek-a-boo game delights most babies. While they don't fully comprehend that they haven't actually disappeared, they find the idea that you don't know where they are a laugh riot! Toss a light blanket or towel over baby's head, wait a moment, and then say, "Where's baby?" a few times. Then lift a corner and say, "There you are! Peek-a-boo!" Soon after learning this game, baby will forego the head covering and will dash away to hide as soon as you say, "Where's baby?"

Tear it up! Believe it or not, many six- to nine-month-old babies delight in watching you perform the simple act of tearing up strips of paper, or even tearing it up themselves once you show them how. Just be watchful so that the paper doesn't make its way to baby's mouth. Don't forget to recycle the paper when you're finished!

LITTLE PIGGIES

Babies love rhymes that involve the tickling of body parts, especially toes. Here's a classic that begins with the big toe and ends with the smallest:

This little piggy went to market,

this little piggy stayed home.

This little piggy had roast beef,

this little piggy had none.

And this little piggy cried,

"Wee, wee, wee," all the way home.

Note: Vegetarians can substitute "tofu" for "roast beef."

Give baby a problem. Give your six- to nine-month-old an object to hold in each hand, then offer her a third object to hold. With repetition, your baby will eventually learn to solve the dilemma by releasing one object to pick up another.

Put action behind the words. Babies eight months old or older love songs accompanied by finger and hand movements that help tell the story. You can probably recall such song-games as Pat-a-Cake and Itsy-Bitsy Spider from your own childhood.

MAKE 'EM LAUGH!

....

Talk silly. Don't underestimate the power of total nonsense! Sing a crazy song of your own creation, with lots of rhyming words and gibberish. Soon you'll be laughing too, which will only add to your baby's glee.

Baby will enjoy this trick over and over, though it may soon tire mom or dad. Fill a small clean spray bottle with cool water. Lightly spritz baby's bare feet when she isn't looking.

ITSY-BITSY SPIDER

The itsy-bitsy spider went up the waterspout.

(Take turns bringing each index finger to the
opposite thumb to imitate the spider
walking up the spout.)

Down came the rain and washed the spider out.

(Wiggle the fingers of both hands while bringing
them down to simulate falling rain.)

Up came the sun and dried up all the rain,

(Raise your arms over your hand
to make a half-circle.)

*And the itsy-bitsy spider went
up the spout again.*

(Repeat the upward walking motion.)

LITTLE BUNNY FOO FOO

....

Little bunny Foo Foo

(Use your index and middle finger of
one hand to make rabbit ears.)

Hopping through the forest

(Make the "bunny" hop.)

Scooping up the field mice

(Scoop up one hand with the opposite hand.)

And bopping them on the head

(Bop the scooped hand with the other.)

*Down came the Good Fairy and she said,
"Little bunny, Foo Foo*

(Use index finger to scold the bunny.)

*I don't want to see you
Scooping up the field mice
And bopping them on the head."*

Give the old Bronx cheer! With baby lying on her back, press your lips to her belly and gently blow through your lips to make them vibrate.

Note: This technique, also known as "blowing a raspberry," works best on a bare belly.

CAUSE AND EFFECT

....

Let your baby see the results of certain actions.

- Turn a light switch on and off.

- Open and close drapes or blinds to reveal the outside world through a window one moment and hide it from view the next.

- Turn the faucet on and off a few times.

- Open and close a drawer or closet door.

- Stop and start the blender to hear the racket it makes.

SETTING A BAD EXAMPLE

....

Let a long strand of linguini or spaghetti dangle from your mouth. Then, with baby watching, slowly suck it into your mouth until it disappears. If you can make the noodle flap from side to side, so much the better.

Baby will find hilarity in the classic bubbles-through-the-straw game. Fill a glass half full of water; then immerse a straw in the water and blow through it.

Note: Baby will eventually learn to imitate this trick and will likely continue this behavior right through junior high school.

Take your baby on a magic carpet ride. Lay her face down on a blanket, rug, or towel, and then drag her around the room by pulling on the blanket. Prewalking babies find this a very amusing way to get around.

Note: Baby should be at least six months old before you try this trick.

TERRIFIC TIP

Show your baby that she is
important to you. Set aside time
each day to give her your
undivided attention.

BUILD SELF-ESTEEM

Nothing influences your child's opinion of himself as much as your opinion of him. Giving your child a positive view of himself right from the start will reap many rewards in the years to come.

Your approval shines like a beacon in your tone of voice, your words, your facial expressions, and your body language — and your disapproval is just as obvious. If something your baby has done displeases you, make sure that you target the behavior, not the child.

Making the decision to have a child is momentous. It is to decide forever to have your heart go walking around outside your body.

— Elizabeth Stone

Help your baby to help himself. Before you know it, he will be learning how spoons, buttons, and doorknobs work. Help him when he truly needs your help, but let him practice and perfect such skills on his own. As a parent, one of your tasks is to teach self-reliance.

Catch your baby in the act of being good. Compliment her when she pets the cat nicely or when she shares her toys with others. If you form this habit while your child is very young, one day you'll be able to say, "Thanks for taking out the garbage without being asked."

TERRIFIC TIP

Show baby respect, so that he'll learn to be respectful. Say "please" and "thank you" to him as often as you do to adults.

READ ALL ABOUT IT

Reading is certainly an enjoyable activity for both you and your baby, but there are other far-reaching benefits to be gained from it. A study conducted at Johns Hopkins University found that babies as young as eight months can recognize and recall words in selected stories repeatedly read to them. Reading to your baby promotes the process of learning language and helps her to develop a vocabulary reserve for her speaking debut later on.

Become familiar with your local library. Many libraries host story hours for different age groups and hold meetings and book signings with guest authors. Most libraries also have an interlibrary loan system that allows you to borrow materials from other libraries that yours does not carry. And, for a gift that truly keeps giving, you can get a library card in your child's name.

Be animated when you read to your baby. Babies absorb word patterns, and they'll remember words and phrases that you get excited about. They'll also learn to interpret meanings from the way you raise or lower your voice.

CAN WE TALK?

....

Sometime between four and six months of age your baby will begin to make deliberate sounds. You might interpret these sounds as merely an exercise of the vocal chords resulting in gibberish, but they are not without meaning. Your baby has been listening to your speech, picking up on subtle variations of tone and pitch, and these early sounds are actually his first attempts at communication. There's so much more to learn!

Talk to your baby. Listen to his babble and respond in kind, mimicking his sounds. This assures him that you're paying attention when he speaks to you.

Build baby's vocabulary. Remember, babies "record" many words from stories and songs and warehouse them for use when they're ready for speech. Point out everyday objects, such as a bottle or teddy bear, and name them for baby.

TERRIFIC TIP

Call things what they are. Use simple words, but use the correct words for objects. For instance, teach her that a cow is a cow, not a "moo-moo."

Songs are a great way to teach the parts of the body. With traditional rhymes such as "This is the way we wash our face," you can reinforce the connection between the label and the body part.

There is a growing trend toward teaching signs to babies to enable them to communicate better sooner. To some degree, we do this automatically. But there is a standard system of simple signs in use that expands a baby's ability to express her ideas and needs. If this idea appeals to you, get a copy of *Baby Signs* by Linda Acredolo and Susan Goodwyn. This book is loaded with examples and an illustrated chart of more than fifty signs.

Note: These signs are not the same as standard sign language.

STAND BACK — LANGUAGE EXPLOSION!

....

One day, usually around her first birthday, your baby will blurt out her first recognizable word. Often this word is "mama," although it may be "ball" or something else. Soon another word comes along, perhaps "dada." Does this mean it's taken a year for your baby to learn two words? Not at all. In fact, she's been busily working on these words and more for months.

However, learning is selective at this stage. While babies as young as 10 months can identify many objects by name, they tend to show much more interest in the names of objects that appeal to them most (ergo, "mama"). Help your baby develop language skills by talking to her about what she's interested in. That includes using her name as a starting point to learn more words. Researchers have found that pairing an infant's name with other words helps the child to learn the words that follow her name. For example, "Alexa's spoon is here." When this exercise is repeated using a variety of new words, your baby will consistently show keener interest in the words that come after her name. The ability to interpret several words at the same time is what scientists refer to as parallel learning.

For the next few months, your baby's brain will become a storehouse of words from which a few are bound to escape verbally now and then. At first, her attempt at speech may sound like gibberish, but she has quite a bit to say. She's not only learning to cross reference objects out loud, she's also learning the names of new objects by using an elimination process. Once she's figured out that the word "spoon" belongs to a spoon and not a fork, the world becomes her oyster — one word at a time.

INTRODUCING...
LEONARDO DA BABY!

·························

At nine months of age, a baby is ready to explore the world of art. But be forewarned: Constant supervision and, at times, an art smock and plenty of towels are necessary to observe safely and preserve your furnishings. Keep soap and water nearby, too.

ARTISTIC ENDEAVORS

....

The next time you sit down to write a letter or pay bills, offer baby a large sheet of paper and a single super-sized, nontoxic crayon. At first he'll stab at the paper, but soon he'll begin to mimic your motions.

Let your baby finger paint with food! Spread out some waxed paper on her high chair tray and offer pudding, mashed potatoes, or oatmeal as edible, no-worry finger paints.

STICK WITH ME, KID!

....

Make stickers out of nontoxic materials and show your older baby how to create mosaic art with them. Using nontoxic paper and markers, draw your sticker designs. Cut out the shapes and brush the backs of them with a mixture of 1 package of flavored gelatin and 2 tablespoons of boiling water. Let the "glue" dry. When licked, the shapes stick to cardboard or paper.

HOMESPUN PLAY CLAY

....

Get into baby sculpture! **Forget modeling clays and "doughs" that can be toxic or may stain fabrics. Using nontoxic ingredients, you can make your own mixtures that are just as fun and colorful.**

> 1 cup flour
>
> 1 cup water
>
> ½ cup salt
>
> 1 tablespoon vegetable oil
>
> 2 teaspoons cream of tartar
>
> food coloring of choice

1. Combine all ingredients in a heavy, nonstick saucepan; mix well. Heat slowly over low heat, stirring constantly.

2. When the mixture forms a ball, turn it onto a clean surface and knead until smooth and elastic. Let cool completely. Store in an airtight container and refrigerate for up to 2 weeks.

NONTOXIC FINGER PAINT

....

If your baby ends up with this homemade "paint" on her face, you won't have to worry about how safe it is. And it washes off easily!

1½ cups cold water

1 cup flour

2 tablespoons salt

1¼ cups hot water

assorted food coloring

1. In a heavy saucepan over low to medium heat, combine cold water, flour, and salt. Using a whisk or rotary beater, beat until a smooth paste forms. Add hot water; boil until mixture thickens.

2. Remove the pan from heat. Add food coloring and beat again until smooth. Make one big batch or divide into portions to make several different colors. Refrigerate unused portions for up to 2 weeks.

YOUR BABY ROCKS!

....

Babies just naturally love music. Although you might have exposed baby to many different beats while he was in utero, he most likely will prefer a specific kind of music once he enters the world. Harvard researchers have found that when babies listened to consonant or melodic music and then heard the same piece with a dissonant arrangement using minor second chords, they showed a distinct preference for the consonant tunes.

In other words, the old adage holds true that soothing music calms the savage breast — or, in this case, your wiggling, restless, stimulation-seeking bundle of energy in a diaper. So make music part of the daily life that you share with your child.

Music does more than entertain; it enhances brain development. A study recently published in *Neurological Research* shows that music training in preschoolers strengthens the spatial and abstract reasoning abilities needed to excel in math and science. Early appreciation of music will boost your budding engineer's chances of success.

BABY'S DAY OUT

Where to go and what to do with baby? Babies love stimulation and learning about the world around them. Here are a few tips for making the most of your afternoons together:

- Make sure baby is fed and well rested before venturing out.

- Dress baby appropriately for the weather.

- Be careful not to overstimulate baby.

- Be prepared to pack up quickly and go home, if necessary.

TAKE A HIKE

....

This is a time when the sling (see page 83) is wonderful to wear in front, so your baby can see what you're seeing instead of where you've been. To prevent injury to either of you, make sure you hike on a clear path, away from rocky ledges and tree branches.

SINGING IN THE RAIN

....

Rainfall is nature's way of cleansing and nourishing the earth. So don your rain gear and take a stroll in the rain. Let baby listen to the symphony raindrops create as they gently fall on your umbrella and on the ground. Or if you prefer, watch the raindrops cascade down a window from indoors.

And don't let a fierce thunderstorm throw your baby into fits — make a point of oohing and aahing at the lightening and laughing at the big booms.

FUN IN THE SUN
(AND THE SAND)

The sights, sounds, and textures of the shore will captivate your baby. Let her feel the sand between her fingers, stroke a seashell, and dip her toes in the water. Just remember to protect her delicate skin from the sun!

TAKE A WALK ON THE WILD SIDE

....

Head for the zoo and see if you can find some baby animals for your own baby to admire. And the day won't be complete unless you mimic the sound each animal makes. Your baby will be entertained and educated, too.

TOUR A MUSEUM

Your baby will find something interesting to look at in any kind of museum, from art to science to natural history. Babies love to look at pictures, so if art is your thing, you can amuse yourself, too — just make sure you can find the exit quickly if your baby doesn't share your enthusiasm for modern art!

It will be gone before you know it. The fingerprints on the wall appear higher and higher. Then suddenly they disappear.

— Dorothy Evslin

CHAPTER 7

PREPARING
FOR THE
FUTURE

CHAPTER 7

It may seem as though your child will be little forever, but she won't. One day she'll set her toys aside and take her first steps toward defining her own identity and her place in the world. Before you know it, she'll be driving a car, picking out a dress for the prom, and perhaps leaving the nest to go to college.

While many factors will contribute to shaping her intellect, academic success, and socialization skills, the actions you take today will help you both prepare for the challenges ahead. You can also preserve the special memories and events of the past and help her to create new ones — now and in the days and years to come.

PREPARING FOR THE FUTURE

Judicious mothers will always keep
in mind that they are the first book
read, and the last put aside, in every
child's library.

— C. Lenox Remond

269

Build your baby a library. Books are one of the most important tools with which to help your child learn about the world. Reading well is also a skill that will bring a lifetime of positive benefits, so it's never too soon to introduce storybooks, poetry, and literature.

Once your child develops a love of reading — and before that, being read to — you'll feel like you never have enough books on hand. Let family and friends know that books are always on baby's (and your) wish list for gift-giving holidays.

RECOMMENDED READING FOR INFANTS

....

These titles are great for babies' first year and many are available in "drool-proof" editions in case they make their way to baby's mouth.

- *Goodnight Moon* by Margaret Wise Brown

- *Where the Wild Things Are* by Maurice Sendak

- *Mad About Madeline* by Ludwig Bemelmans

- *Curious George's ABCs* by H. A. Rey and Margaret Rey

- *Clifford the Big Red Dog* by Norman Bridwell

- *The Runaway Bunny* by Margaret Wise Brown

- *White on Black* by Tana Hoban

- *Jamberry* by Bruce Degen

- *Brown Bear, Brown Bear, What Do You See?* by Bill Martin Jr. and Eric Carle

- *The Snowy Day* by Ezra Jack Keats

- *Guess How Much I Love You* by Sam McBratney and Anita Jeram

- *Love You Forever* by Robert Munsch and Sheila McGraw

MAKING MEMORIES

....

Start a daily journal, or continue writing in the diary you started during your pregnancy. You'll be up at rather odd times during the night, so you might as well put to good use those moments when you're not nursing. A journal of your thoughts and feelings at this time will be something very special to share with your child years from now. My tattered journal still gets pulled from the bookshelf now and then, even 22 years later!

TERRIFIC TIP

While you'll want to capture on film
(both still and video) such events
as baby's first birthday or holiday,
don't forget day-to-day events like
bath time, snuggling with her older
brother, or those moments when she's
a sleeping angel.

THE WAY WE WERE

Keep a scrapbook. Unlike a photo album, scrapbooks contain "scraps" of past events and occasions. You'll want to fill it with items such as the birth announcement, the bill for your hospital or birthing room (you'll both get a real kick out of this later, believe me), and a snip of hair from baby's first haircut.

Keep a memory box. Use this to hold baby booties, favorite toys, early works of art, and all the little trinkets he held so dear from his childhood. You're sure to receive lots of "welcome baby" cards upon your baby's arrival. Keep them to share with your child when he's old enough to be curious about the day he was born.

Order a time capsule kit that allows family members to write "letters to the future" and includes a book in which to record what life was like way back when.

Write your family's story. Create a special book or album using a combination of photos, scrapbooking, and journaling techniques to record your family's history and cultural heritage. If possible, include a family tree that displays as many generations as you can. Ask an elder in the family to help to provide this information. If you still need to fill in a few gaps, there are numerous genealogy Web sites where you may be able to search birth, marriage, and death records relevant to your family.

Go digital. Creating a digital photo album is easy to do these days, with plenty of layout designs and themes available to download from the Internet or with purchased software. Digital albums can be easily decorated with graphics and you can insert your own quotes or favorite sayings to illustrate each photograph. Digital albums are also easy to share with friends and family through e-mail and can be updated at any time.

Make your own holiday greetings. Gather the family together for an annual portrait to use for holiday photo greeting cards. It's a great way to send a personalized message to friends and family, especially those who live far away. It's also a fun way to capture how much your family grows and changes throughout the years.

ORGANIZE A "PLAY" GROUP

....

Babies bring people together! You can meet other parents with babies through friends, neighbors, church, work, or at the local park or library. Infants under a year old don't really play with each other, but gatherings can provide much needed respite for parents. Plan on being together for about one to two hours, once or twice a week.

Or arrange your gatherings so that two or three parents watch a couple of extra babies, allowing the others a chance to have a quiet lunch out or run a few errands without a baby in tow.

TERRIFIC TIP

Set up a toy swap with your
playgroup to exchange toys that
your baby is tired of with fun new
items. In a few weeks, you can swap
them back again!

IT'S NEVER TOO EARLY

....

Start a custodial savings account for your baby. You'll be surprised at how much small, regular contributions can add up over the long haul. If you put just $10 into this fund each week, your child will have over $9,000 before interest when she is 18 years of age. If you deposit $25 into her account each week, she'll have more than $23,000 — a good start toward college tuition or a business venture.

Whenever you are able to, pad your child's nest egg with bonus payments. These extra deposits might come from tax refunds, inheritance benefits, annuity payments, monetary gifts from family and friends, and so on.

Start your estate planning now. **Most** people don't give a lot of thought to estate planning until they get older. However, your child is your most important "asset," regardless of how much money or property you have. In addition to having a will drawn up, you should also prepare a Letter of Intent. This legal document outlines your specific instructions to a court or child advocate in the event that you are not able to care for your child, including your preference in appointing a guardian.

Save your change. If you took the leftover change made from buying that latte on your way to work every morning and dropped it into a coffee can each night, you'd be amazed at how quickly it can add up. Get yourself some coin wrappers and have a ball rolling up your spare quarters, dimes, nickels, and even pennies to deposit into your child's savings account later. When your child is old enough to help you, you'll be setting a wise example.

Be sure your life, disability, and mortgage (if applicable) insurance policies are up-to-date. After all, you'd want your baby to be provided for if something happened to you. If you don't have any kind of insurance, what are you waiting for?

LET UNCLE SAM HELP OUT

....

Each state in the United States offers 529 programs designed to help families pay for college. With a *529 College Savings Plan*, the funds are exempt from federal income tax as well as state tax in many states. The money saved is invested in stocks, bonds, and money market funds and can still be supplemented by financial aid in the future.

A 529 Prepaid College Tuition Program is also exempt from federal tax and is usually deductible from state tax liability and offers additional benefits over the savings plan. For one thing, the money invested assures that parents can purchase the tuition in advance at today's cost.

For another, there is less risk since the money isn't being invested in stocks. However, both plans stipulate that the invested funds must be used toward college tuition and related expenses affiliated with a public college or university within your state of residency.

Make the branches of your family tree strong, but allow them to bend. Your child may represent the next generation, but his core values and ethics will be rooted in yesterday. While you share with your child the heritage and traditions that your family honors, help him to develop an appreciation and respect for those observed by families different from your own.

Exposing baby to different cultures from a very early age — whether through stories or first-hand experiences — will help to instill the values of diversity and tolerance. Remember, too, that nothing will affect baby more in this regard than your own outlook and actions toward others.

Perhaps the best thing about the future is that it only comes one day at a time.

— Dean Acheson

RESOURCES

....

PUBLICATIONS

Mothering magazine: *www.mothering.com*

Working Mother magazine: *www.workingmother.com*

BREAST-FEEDING INFORMATION

Lamaze International: *www.lamaze.org*

MUMS National Parent-to-Parent Network
www.netnet.net/mums

ADVOCATES OF PVC-FREE PLASTIC AND TOYS

Greenpeace: *www.greenpeace.org*

Health Child Healthy World: *http://healthychild.org*

DIAPERS

All Together Enterprises: *www.clothdiaper.com*

ClothDiapers.com: *www.clothdiapers.com*

gDiapers: *www.gdiapers.com*

The Hain Celestial Group: *www.tushies.com*

Punkin-Butt: *www.punkinbutt.com*

SLINGS AND MAYA WRAPS

BabySling.com: *http://babysling.com*

New Native Inc.: *www.newnativebaby.com*

ORGANIC CLOTHING AND BEDDING

A Happy Planet: *www.ahappyplanet.com*

Green Babies Inc.: *www.greenbabies.com*

NaturalEco Organics: *www.naturaleco.com*

FUTONS AND BASSINETS

Blue Horizon Organics: *www.babyhollow.com*

White Lotus Homes: *www.whitelotus.net*

NATURAL PAINTS, FINISHES, STAINS, AND FLOORING

BioShield Healthy Living Store: *www.bioshieldpaint.com*

The Old Fashioned Milk Paint Co.: *www.milkpaint.com*

Planetary Solutions: *www.planetearth.com*

NATURAL VITAMINS AND MEDICINES

Herbs for Kids: *www.herbsforkids.com*

Native Remedies: *www.nativeremedies.com*

ORGANIC FOODS

Earthbound Farm: *www.ebfarm.com*

Earth's Best Organic
    The Hain Celestial Group: *www.earthsbest.com*

NATURAL BABY SOAPS AND LOTIONS

Erbaviva: *www.erbaviva.com*

Magick Botanicals: *www.magickbotanicals.com*

Our Natural Baby: *www.ournaturalbaby.com*

Trusted Care
    NaturaSales: *www.trustedcare.com*

Weleda International: *www.weleda.com*

NATURAL TOYS

All Natural Baby: *www.allnaturalbaby.com*

Peapods : *www.peapods.com*

Eco-Wise: *www.ecowise.com*

MUSIC AND VIDEOS

BabyCenter: *http://store.babycenter.com*

Genius Babies: *www.geniusbabies.com*

Hap-Pal Music, Inc.: *www.happalmer.com*

Infant Learning Company: *www.infantlearning.com*

MISCELLANEOUS

College Savings Bank: *www.collegesavingsbank.com*

INDEX

OTHER STOREY TITLES
YOU WILL ENJOY

Knit Baby Blankets!, **edited by Gwen Steege.**
Fifteen easy-to-follow patterns to create heirloom pieces
any newborn's parents will treasure.
128 pages. Die-cut hardcover. ISBN 978-1-58017-495-4.

Knit Baby Head & Toes!, **edited by Gwen Steege.**
Jaunty caps, stylish socks, sweet little booties: 15 patterns
to create distinctive, irresistible accessories.
128 pages. Die-cut hardcover. ISBN 978-1-58017-494-7.

Organic Body Care Recipes, **by Stephanie Tourles.**
Homemade, herbal formulas for glowing skin, hair, and
nails, plus a vibrant self.
384 pages. Paper. ISBN 978-1-58017-676-7.

Natural BabyCare, **by Colleen K. Dodt.**
Pure and soothing herbal recipes and techniques to
promote the health of mothers and babies.
160 pages. Paper. ISBN 978-0-88266-953-3.

Rosemary Gladstar's Herbal Remedies for Children's Health.
How to use herbs such as chamomile, lemon balm, and
echinacea to create gentle baby care products and safe
treatments for childhood illnesses.
80 pages. Paper. ISBN 978-1-58017-153-3.

These and other books from Storey Publishing are available
wherever quality books are sold or by calling 1-800-441-5700.
Visit us at *www.storey.com.*